think
like a pony
IN THE SADDLE

STEP 1 WORKBOOK

Lynn Henry

www.thinklikeapony.co.uk

THINK LIKE A PONY PUBLISHING

Published in Great Britian in 2010 by
Think Like A Pony Publishing

© Lynn Henry, 2010

All rights reserved. No part of this publication may be reproduced, stored in a retrieval system, or transmitted in any form or by any means, electronic, mechanical, photocopying, recording or otherwise, without the written permission of the publisher.

British Library Catalogue in Publication Data
A catalogue record for this book is available from the British Library.

ISBN 978-0-9566591-0-1

Disclaimer of Liability
The author and publisher shall have neither liability nor responsibility to any person or entity with respect to any loss or damage caused directly or indirectly by the information contained in this book. While the book is as accurate as the author can make it, there may be errors, omissions and inaccuracies.

Think Like A Pony Publishing
Tel: 0044 (0)778 213 2649
Website: www.thinklikeapony.co.uk

Acknowledgements

I would like to thank my family and friends for the important part that they have played in helping me to produce this book.

Thank you to my husband Ged for all of your love and support!!

Thank you to my children for being patient and photogenic.

Thank you to Sarah Gibbon, without whom this book would have never made it past pen and paper.

Thank you again to Su Smith who creates such wonderful illustrations that capture the imagination of everyone.

Thank you Chris Bee, I have truly found a friend in you.

Thank you to all the children, ponies and horses that have inspired and compelled me to continue the Think Like a Pony Series. I so hope that you enjoy them and they help you on your journey to understanding ponies.

Written by: Lynn Henry

Illustrated by: Su Smith

Photography by: Lynn Henry and Ruth Young

Design by: Chris Bee

think
like a pony
IN THE SADDLE

STEP 1 WORKBOOK

CONTENTS		PAGE
	Introduction	**6**
Chapter 1	Becoming a leader	8
Chapter 2	The saddle	13
Chapter 3	The bridle	22
Chapter 4	Learning to use the reins	32
Chapter 5	Where is your weight?	42
Chapter 6	Putting on the saddle	51
Chapter 7	Putting on the bridle	61
Chapter 8	Following the feel of the bridle	70
Chapter 9	Getting on and off your pony	81
Chapter 10	Flexing	90
Chapter 11	Sitting in balance	98
Chapter 12	Walk on and stop	109
Chapter 13	Moving together	123
Chapter 14	Using your body language to direct your pony	134
Chapter 15	Moving backwards	142
Chapter 16	Obstacles and challenges	151

ABOUT THE AUTHOR

Lynn Henry is an instructor of horsemanship, both on the ground and ridden. She lives in West Yorkshire, England, with her husband and four children.

A dedicated senior school teacher before leaving to bring up her family of three boys and a girl, Lynn has had a lifelong passion for teaching and particularly the teaching of children.

Lynn came to the horse world relatively late in life (35) as a result of helping her children to learn about ponies and riding and was immediately captivated by the relationship between human and pony. She has since dedicated 14 years to horse psychology, with particular emphasis on building a strong foundation on which to develop better understanding, harmony and friendship between pony and student.

Forever in pursuit of a holistic approach to horses, Lynn has added shiatsu for horses and iridology for horses to her list of ever-widening skills.

FORWARD
by Jim Dukes

The bond between horse and rider goes back thousands of years. In order to enjoy this bond to the full you have to learn to understand and communicate with horses.

Much of modern riding instruction is based on methods used to teach soldiers to ride in the cavalry. I sometimes feel that this can result in a belief that you need to dominate the horse to control him rather than trying to see things from the horse's perspective first. Lynn Henry was not formally taught to ride herself before she first took her children for lessons. However, whilst watching their beginner lessons, she felt that empathy and understanding with the horse were not developed early enough in the process.

In her Think Like a Pony workbook series, Lynn has really thought about how horses or ponies think, and she uses this to teach children and adults how to communicate effectively with horses. By breaking the communication down into really simple steps beginners can learn from the outset how to truly bond with the horse.

However, although aimed at less experienced riders, I think almost anyone who rides can learn something from this book. I also think that anyone who teaches riding at any level should read the book as it will provide a fresh insight to teaching. I particularly liked the chapter on balance and the emphasis right through the book of how the way the rider sits and moves their body affects the ability of the horse to be able to move. The idea of pairing up with someone and seeing how the way you move affects them being the horse is a new concept to me. I think this makes it really easy to understand how your weight, movement and balance can affect the horse.

The workbook format is carefully thought out, well illustrated, clear and easy to follow and detailed. It is easy to refer back to any points you want to refresh and should help to set a solid foundation for a lifetime's enjoyment with horses.

Jim Dukes BVM&S, MRCVS vet and polo trainer.

Introduction

When you look at the world through the eyes of a pony, you can understand:
- How they think
- Why they act the way they do
- What is important to them

Time spent with a pony should be safe and fun and this can be achieved if you use a language that you both understand. Through this understanding you can communicate with a pony and form a friendship so they can become a willing and happy partner.

Before you ride your pony try to 'Think Like a Pony'.
What does it feel like to have someone on your back, asking you to go, stop and turn? What does it feel like to wear a saddle or bridle?
By thinking like a pony you can learn to make riding fun for both you and your pony.
If you can learn to understand how to ride in harmony with a pony, riding can become easy, natural, fun and above all safe.
A thinking rider is a safe rider.
A thinking pony is a safe pony.

To parents or guardians:
Children should be supervised at all times. It is important that before a child rides a pony, the pony must be:

1. **Accepting of the child and saddle.**
2. **Controllable and willing to yield to pressure.**
3. **Confident and able to relax in his environment.**

This preparation should take place before you ride. By working with your pony on the ground you can build respect, trust and confidence, so that all the experiences you have together are safe and fun.
The **Think Like a Pony** series helps you, through understanding the world through a pony's eyes, to ride naturally and in harmony with your pony. For more information please visit the Think Like a Pony website at **www.thinklikeapony.co.uk**

1

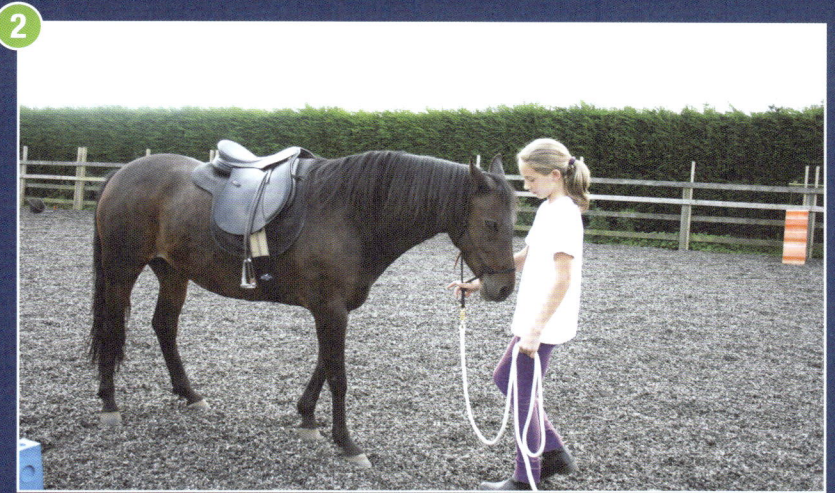

2

3

Chapter 1
Becoming a leader

The most important thing from your pony's point of view is that he can respect and trust you. To trust you, your pony must be able to understand you and be capable of doing what you are asking of him. Your pony must see you as a leader, someone that he can believe in and have fun with. This relationship, built on respect, trust and communication, begins on the ground. The **Think Like a Pony on the ground** series shows you how to start building this relationship with a pony.
Once you start to ride a pony the relationship between you both is very important.
It is essential that you can trust your pony and that your pony can trust you on the ground and on his back.

> Sitting on a pony's back may seem simple to you, but from your pony's perspective you could be a predator ready to attack.

do I trust you?

yes I do!

> He has to trust you and know that you are a good leader who will keep him safe, and that you will not hurt him.

When you are riding your pony he is very aware of your intention and body language. He has to make sense of what you are asking him to do. When you ride your pony remember that YOU are the leader and you must keep your intention on what you are doing. When you are riding if you are thinking about one thing and asking him to do another thing, he will become confused, afraid or take over.

If you are not being a good leader he will sense and feel it.
If you are thoughtful and keep your intention on riding, you will learn to become determined, calm and clear, showing your pony that you are a good leader, even in a difficult situation.

Ponies are sensitive creatures and they have emotions and feelings. By watching a pony's body language you can try to understand how they are feeling about a situation.
They may not express their emotions the same as you but they still have feelings.
They can feel:
- Afraid
- Unsure
- Confused
- Content
- Joyous
- Lonely
- Relaxed

A good leader cares.
By listening to your pony and watching their body language you can show that you are a caring leader. You must still be aware of your pony's body language and try to understand what he is feeling and thinking when you are riding just like you do when you are on the ground.
Is he:

- **Afraid?**
- **In pain?**
- **Unsure?**
- **Trying to be the leader?**

When you can understand what your pony is trying to communicate to you then you can:
- **Build his confidence**   • **Sort out his pain**   • **Be a better leader**

Always be aware of your thoughts, intention and body language if you want to communicate effectively with your pony. If you want your pony to give you his attention and listen to you, you must give your attention to your pony and listen to him.
Learning to communicate with your pony effectively will help you to become a good leader when you ride him.

This way you can:
- Help him to make the correct response.
- Avoid confusion, frustration or fear.

A good leader would care and ask:
- "What can I do for my pony?"
- "What can we do together?"

A poor leader would be selfish and ask:
- "What can my pony do for me?"

It is always too easy to blame your pony if things go wrong. Practise staying calm in any situation where you may be angry, upset, scared or confused. Relax by breathing out slowly, this will help you to slow down and think before you do or say something you may regret. This will help you to think about the situation. You may even react differently! This will help you to become a better leader for your pony.
As a good leader, it is up to you to show your pony that being with you and doing things together is fun. When you both work together as a team it feels good.

Before you ride

A pony loves the touch of his special friend and you can learn more about how to touch a pony in the **Think Like a Pony on the ground** series.

Stroke or massage your pony, watching his body language so that you can find out how he is feeling. Your pony will let you know if you are too rough or too quick so watch his body language signals.

This pony is concerned **This pony is relaxed**

Your touch is reassuring and helps to build a bond between you and your pony and is another way to help him to relax. Touching your pony all over his body in a way that he likes helps to build his confidence in you.

Feel or look for any tight spots. You can use your rub like a massage to relax any sore or tight muscles. When you feel a muscle that needs a rub, be as gentle or firm as your pony needs. Try to 'Think like a pony'. What pressure do they use when rubbing each other? What pressure would you like if someone was to massage your tight or sore muscles?

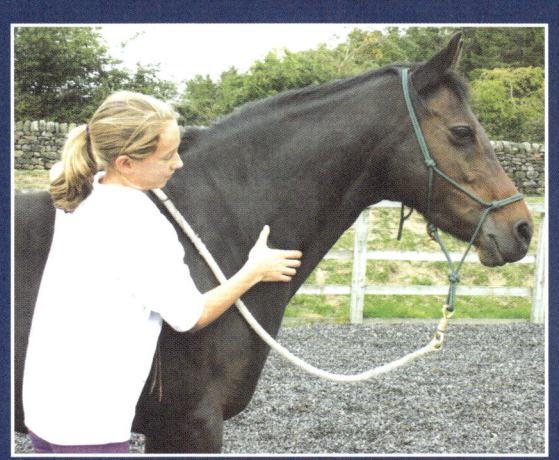

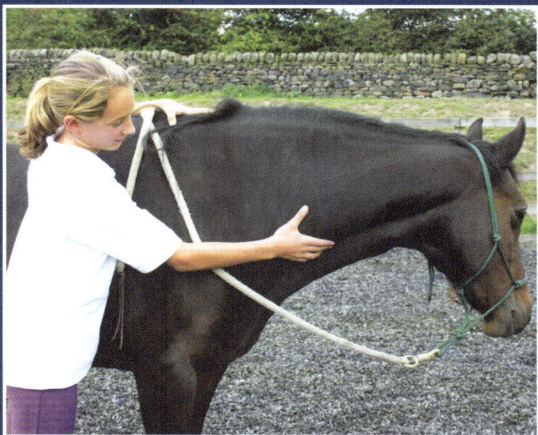

Asking your pony to stretch

Stretching his neck forward and down encourages him to lift and stretch his back. This is excellent preparation for riding and also shows you how he should lift his back to support you in the saddle.

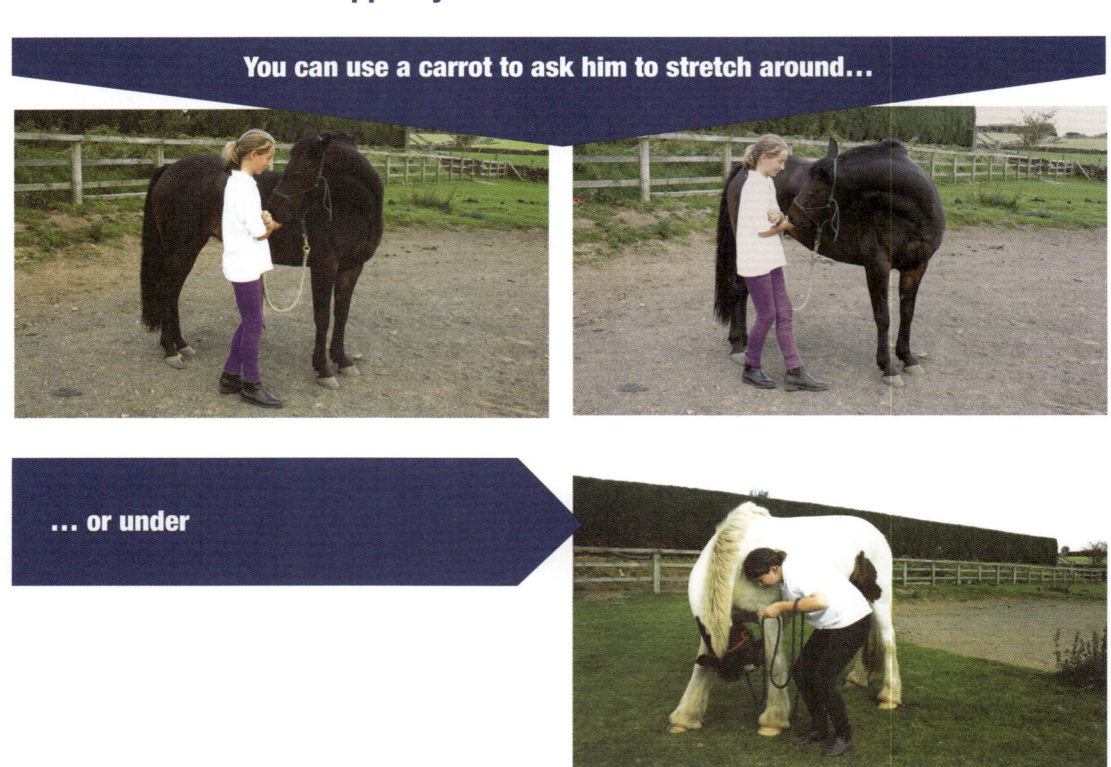

You can use a carrot to ask him to stretch around…

… or under

If he is stiff he may not be able to stretch as far, but if you are patient and consistent he will improve. Go slowly and build up his confidence.
Be consistent and encourage him to stretch for the carrot.
Massaging and stretching your pony are great preparation for riding. Try to make time before and after you ride to massage and stretch your pony.

Chapter 2
The saddle

The saddle is essential tack and must fit your pony so that he feels comfortable and relaxed wearing it.

Think like a pony, if you had to wear a saddle what would you like? What would be important to you?

The saddle and its parts

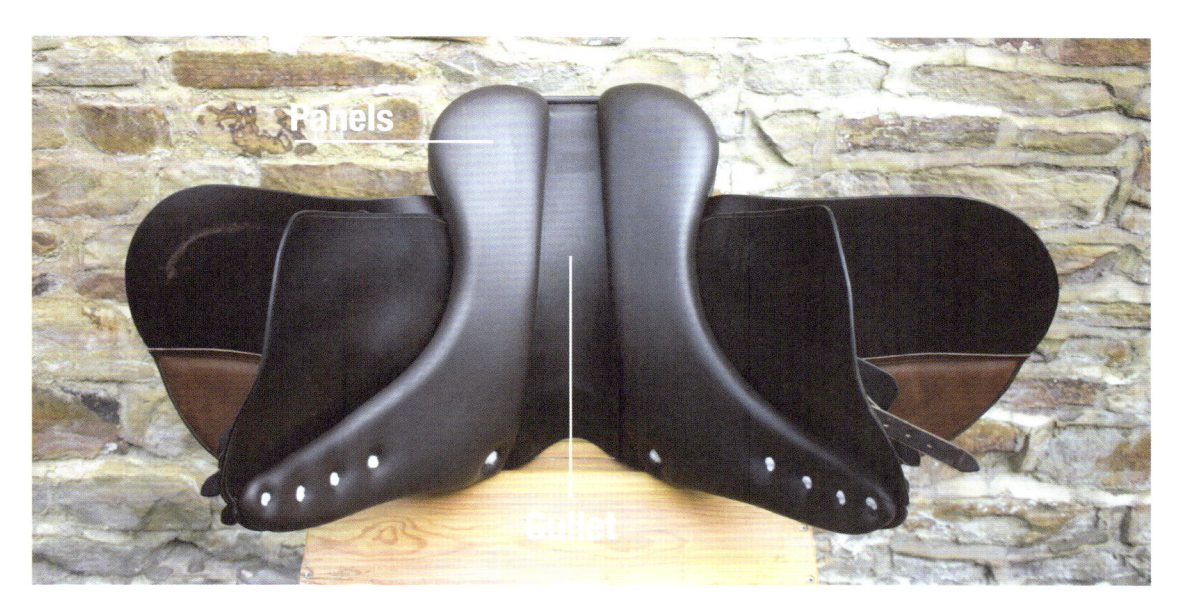

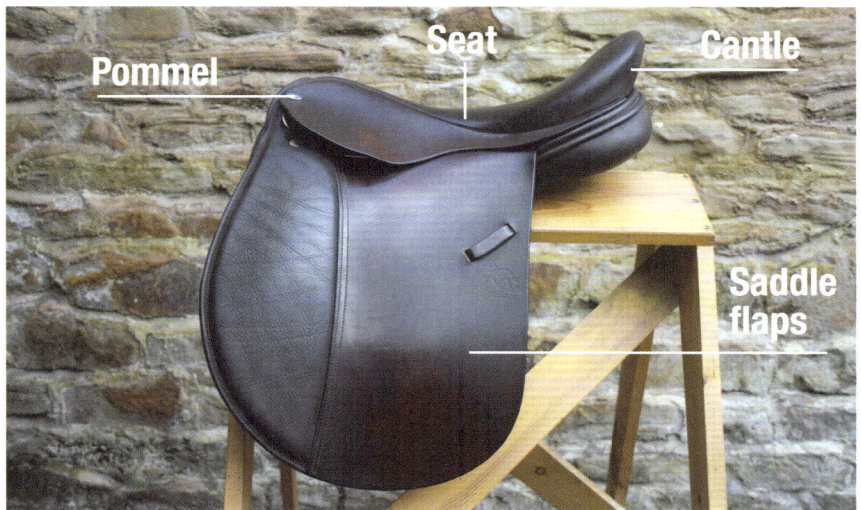

Panels

Gullet

Pommel — *Seat* — *Cantle*

Saddle flaps

13

What to look for in your pony's saddle

Is the saddle wide enough?
Wearing a saddle is like wearing a comfortable pair of shoes that you could wear all day.
- **They would not pinch or hurt.**
- **You could wear a pair of socks inside to make them extra comfortable.**
- **There would be room for your toes to wiggle.**

You may not know what it feels like to wear a tight uncomfortable saddle, but imagine what it would feel like wearing a pair of tight uncomfortable shoes.

Your pony's saddle should be wide enough to allow him to move. If he cannot move freely he will begin to 'shrink' away from the tight saddle and because of this the muscle behind his shoulders and over his back will sink away! He may hold his head high and dip his back to try to move away from the saddle.

If the saddle is not wide enough he may not want to move forward or he may move very quickly trying to get away from the saddle.

A tight-fitting saddle can cause deep bruising and muscle wastage, especially behind the shoulder and wither.

A saddle which is too tight at any point will cause your pony to become sore and uncomfortable.

A pony-shaped saddle is U shaped.
A narrow saddle is V shaped.

Some pony's saddles are so narrow that the pony becomes the shape of his saddle! Depending upon a pony's personality he may react to his tight saddle and become cross or give in and become quiet and depressed.

The saddle panels

The panels of your saddle should protect your pony's back from your bony bottom. The gullet must be wide enough so that no pressure is put on his spine. The gullet for ponies should be 1.5 to 2 inches and 2.5 inches for horses from front to back and should flare out wider at the front pommel of the saddle. If the gullet is too narrow, it will pinch your pony's spine and can damage nerves and muscle causing him to be very sore and uncomfortable.

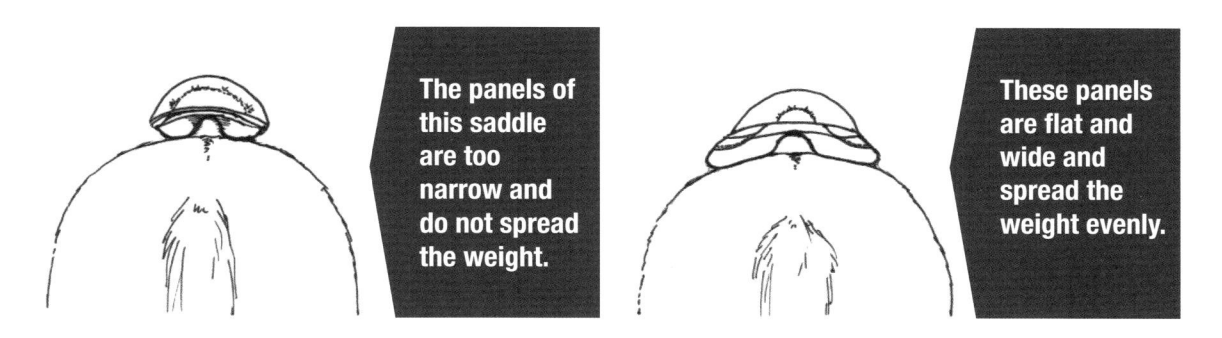

The panels of this saddle are too narrow and do not spread the weight.

These panels are flat and wide and spread the weight evenly.

The panels of the saddle should be flat and wide enough to spread your weight as evenly as possible over your pony's back. If they are too narrow or too hard they cannot do this. Check the panels of your saddle to make sure they are even and lump free. If they are not you should seek professional advice.

Your saddle panels should touch your pony's back along the full length and width of the panel, so that your weight can be spread evenly. They act like a cushion. Sometimes if your pony is uncomfortable in the saddle, when you take the saddle off, there is a depression on his back which matches the shape of his saddle. This shows you that he is not comfortable in his saddle.

Are the saddle panels soft enough?

The saddle panels should be soft to touch so that your pony can move his back underneath them. Hard panels do not give and may restrict his movement or make him sore.

Feel the panels of your pony's saddle. You should be able to push them in with a little pressure.

Even if the saddle panels are soft to touch, your pony will also need a numnah or a thick saddle cloth to give him extra cushioning and protection.

The numnah should be shaped to fit over his withers and into the gullet of your saddle. This way, when he moves, the numnah will not pull down and put pressure on his withers.

A good numnah will have a fleece lining for comfort and absorption of sweat.

Try this: Understanding the importance of the saddle panels

With a partner

1. Put your thumb on the top of your partner's shoulder where the neck meets the body.
2. Gently and slowly start to apply a little bit of steady pressure. Notice how they feel and react.
3. Now with your hand flat, start to gently and slowly apply pressure in the same place. Notice how they feel and react.

Swap over so you can feel steady pressure from a thumb and a flat hand on the top of your shoulder.
Discuss these feelings and reactions.

When you use your thumb you are using a small surface area which puts more pressure on one area.
When using your hand it is a larger surface area, which spreads the effect of the pressure.

This is what the panels of your saddle do when you sit on your pony's back.

They spread out the weight of your bony bum!

Feel your bony bum

- Sit upright on a hard chair.
- **A** Put your hand under your bum.
- Can you feel the bones which you sit on?

These are your 'Seat Bones'.

- **B** Try rocking forwards and backwards or wiggling.
- While you are sitting on your hands was it comfortable?
- Now try this sitting on a cushion.

If you were a pony would you like a protection from these 'seat bones'?

Is the saddle the correct shape?

If your saddle sits over your pony's shoulders he will be uncomfortable because the saddle will restrict the movement of his shoulder blade causing him pain. This will prevent him from moving his front legs correctly.

The saddle should be shaped to allow him to move his shoulders freely. If they can't he may shorten his stride or even become lame.

This saddle is shaped to allow the pony's shoulder to move and fit a saddle cloth comfortably underneath.

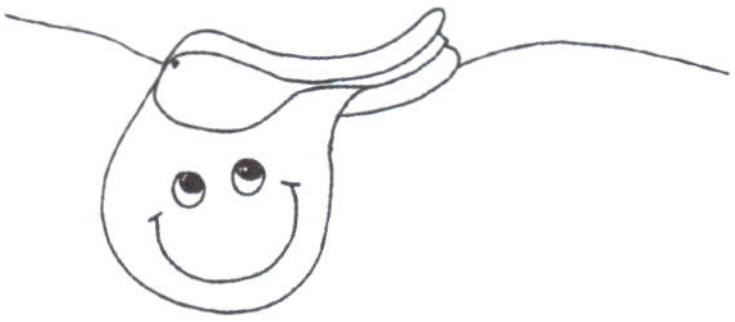

This saddle is shaped too far forward and is stopping the pony's shoulder moving freely.

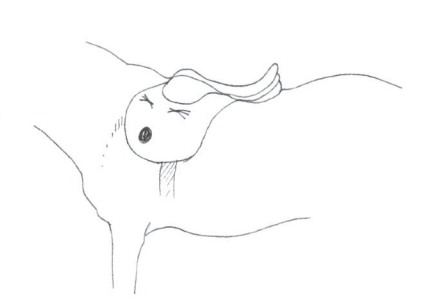

Is the saddle the correct length?

Your saddle should not be too long for your pony and must sit on his rib cage so that his delicate organs such as kidneys (and in mares, ovaries) are protected.

This saddle is too long.

This saddle is the correct length and shape for this pony and can fit a saddle cloth comfortably underneath.

To find the end of your pony's ribcage feel down his side for the end of his ribs. The narrowest part of him is just at the end of his ribcage, in front of his hips and back legs. This is where his delicate organs are.

This girl is first finding the end of her pony's rib cage.

Then she is checking that there is space behind her pony's saddle.

Check you have space behind your saddle to avoid putting pressure on delicate organs.

Is your saddle level?

When you put the saddle in the correct place on your pony, it is important to look at the seat. This is the **middle point** and is where you will sit.

Is this point flat?

If the saddle causes you to tip backwards, you would put more pressure behind his saddle. This will cause him pain and discomfort. Your pony will find it difficult to lift his back or place his hind legs underneath himself.

If your saddle tips forwards when you sit on it, you would put more pressure on his shoulders causing pain and damage to the muscles there. Your pony would shrink his back away from his saddle and may raise his head and neck in anticipation of pain.

Make sure that your saddle does not rock backwards or forwards. To check if your saddle moves put one hand on the pommel and one hand on the cantle. Can you make it rock? If you can it will rock backwards or forwards when you sit on it and cause your pony to be uncomfortable.

This saddle is rocking which can cause the pony to be sore in front of the wither and around the cantle.

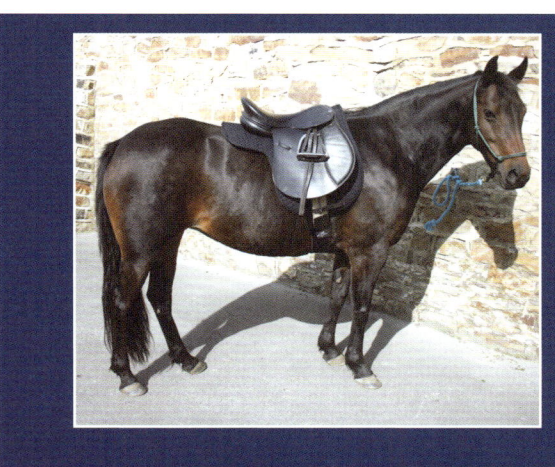

Soft pads can be used to help lift or balance a saddle so that it sits level.

When a pony is **alert** or **tense** he will raise his head and hollow his back.
When a pony is **relaxed** he will lower his head and his back is soft.

You want to ride a relaxed pony so that it is a good experience for you both.

Check your pony's saddle regularly. Like you, your pony changes size and shape. Ponies often change shape when they lose weight, develop their muscles or get older. Therefore you should check the fit of your saddle and girth regularly.

The wrong saddle can cause huge problems. They make a pony weak and 'lazy'. If you are unsure or need more professional help, visit my website www.thinklikeapony.co.uk.

The girth, stirrup leathers and irons

The saddle is held in place by a girth. Remember that like the saddle the girth needs to be the correct size and comfortable for your pony to wear. A padded leather girth gives the best comfort and fit.

The stirrup irons need to be the correct width for your foot. If the stirrup irons are too wide, your foot could slip through them. If they are too small, you will not be able to put your foot in the stirrup correctly or you could get your foot stuck. It is a good idea to think about using safety stirrups when you are riding to help keep you safe.

The stirrups are attached to the saddle with stirrup leathers. Your stirrup leathers need to be adjustable, so that they can be the correct length for you. If your stirrups are not the correct length it will make it hard for you to balance.

Here is a checklist to help you to see if your pony's saddle is comfortable. If your pony shows more than one of these signs or symptoms on a regular basis then look at his saddle fit.

1. Pulling unpleasant faces when you appear with his tack.
2. Refusing to accept the bit or bridle.
3. Moving away from the tack.
4. Shrinking or dipping his back away from the saddle when you put it on or try to mount up.
5. Kicking out or biting when the saddle is put on or girthed up.
6. Refusing to stand still or pawing the ground when you try to mount.
7. Refusing to move or unwilling to walk, trot, canter or jump.
8. Finding stopping difficult.
9. Running backwards.
10. Rearing.
11. Bucking.
12. Shying or spooking.
13. Unwilling to stretch when you ride him.
14. Riding with his head in the air and his back hollow or his hind legs trailing.
15. Rushing or pulling.
16. Unwilling to turn or bend.
17. Short choppy strides.
18. Refusing to be caught.
19. Tight over-developed neck muscles.
20. Tight, sore back and hamstrings.

Chapter 3
The bridle

When you ride, the bridle helps you to communicate clearly and effectively with your pony, just like a line and halter does on the ground. When you use the bridle, you must understand how it works so that you can use it sensitively and give clear instructions to your pony. Not all bridles have a bit, some are called 'bitless bridles' but they are used in a similar way and must fit your pony correctly.

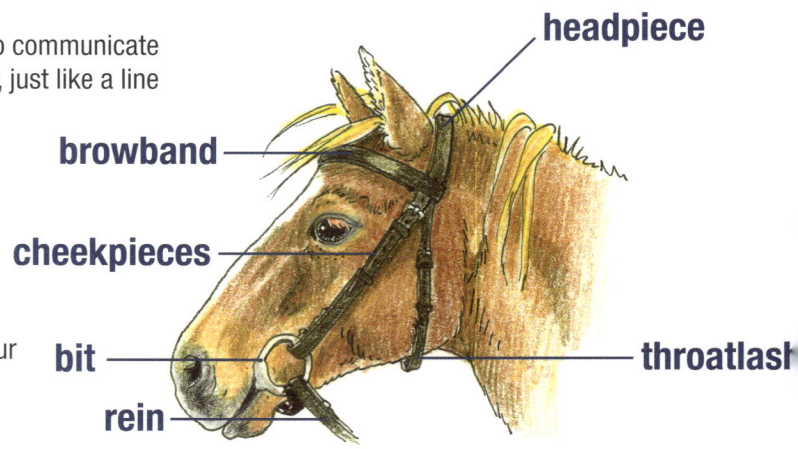

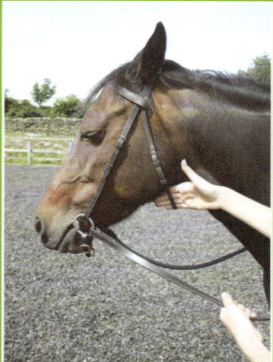

- headpiece
- browband
- cheekpieces
- bit
- rein
- throatlash

The throatlash should be fastened so your pony has enough room to move his head. If it is too loose his bridle can come off. Allow one hand's width, as shown.

Some ponies wear a lip strap to stop the bit slipping through their mouth.

If the browband is too tight it will cause your pony to have a headache. If it is too loose it will irritate him and not hold his bridle in place. His bit will not hang in the correct place if his bridle is not fitted correctly.

For the bit or bridle to be effective and direct your pony he must be able to move his head and neck freely. To do this he must be able to move his lower jaw freely. Where your pony looks, the rest of his body should follow.

For example:
When you move the right rein this in turn moves the right side of the bit or bridle. This in turn asks your pony to move his jaw and head to the right. Where he looks to the right the rest of his body should follow.

Your pony's teeth

His teeth must allow his jaw to move side to side and backwards and forwards.

Like your pony you can move your lower jaw. Your lower jaw moves side to side and backwards and forwards. When you lower your head and neck, your lower jaw slides forwards. When you raise your head your lower jaw slides backwards. This is the same for your pony.

Your pony has a set amount of permanent tooth growth. His teeth will grow down and wear away as he eats through his life. Older ponies will eventually wear away all of their teeth and then may lose them.

In the wild a pony eats tough grasses and even shrubs which constantly wear away his teeth! What your pony eats everyday may not be what he needs to keep wearing his teeth down.

If his teeth do not wear down they may develop sharp edges, which are painful against the inside of his cheek. These sharp edges can stop his jaw from moving correctly side to side or backwards and forwards.

If your pony cannot move his jaw freely he cannot turn his head comfortably, and he will not be able to follow the feel of the bridle. Your pony will resist the bit and bridle and may become tense through his body. This is not an enjoyable experience for either of you.

A pony whose teeth are uncomfortable often has a headache. Think like a pony. How would you feel, if your mouth was sore, or it was difficult to move your jaw?

If your pony is uncomfortable around his head, he may try to avoid your touch. For example:
- **Raise his head and neck.**
- **Lower his head and neck.**
- **Shake his head and neck.**
- **Back away.**
- **Walk away.**

At least once a year you must ask a vet or a registered horse dentist to check your pony's teeth. Visit my website for further information.

You can prepare your pony for putting his bridle on by checking:
- **He has had his teeth looked at and they are not causing him pain.**
- **He can confidently lower his head and neck from a feel of steady pressure from his halter, or your arm over his neck.**
- **He can confidently allow you to stroke his head and ears.**

REMEMBER to use approach and retreat around this sensitive area to build his confidence in your touch. Massage any tight or sore muscles.

Massage his ears, like the young girl in the picture. This is an excellent way to relieve tension and headaches and build a bond between you and your pony.

The bit
A pony's mouth is very sensitive and if you use a bridle with a bit then it is important to remember this is a very sensitive area. There are many different kinds of bits to suit the different shapes and sizes of ponies mouths and tongues. If you choose a bit that does not suit your pony you can cause him to feel afraid and anxious. He may:
- Lean on the bit.
- Have difficulty turning.
- Try to spit the bit out.
- Refuse to close his mouth.
- Stick out his tongue or put his tongue over the bit.
- Flap his lip or hold his mouth tight.
- Lift his head in the air.
- Rear or run backwards.
- Find it difficult to swallow.

These are just some of the signs that you may see if a pony is uncomfortable. If your pony is anxious or afraid of his bit, this can also cause pain and problems in the rest of his body.
If you need any help or advice on choosing the correct bit, visit my website.

Where does the bit sit?
There is a natural gap in your pony's mouth where there are no teeth. This is where the bit sits.

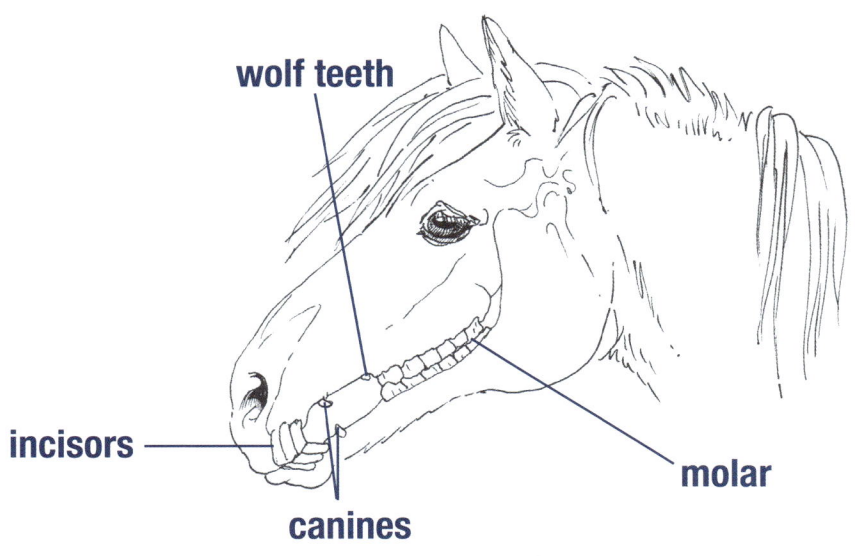

The front teeth are called incisors; the back teeth are called molars.
Some ponies may also have wolf teeth or canine teeth.
Wolf teeth are the first premolars which usually only appear on the upper jaw. Canine teeth appear more in male ponies.
It is important that the bit does not bang or catch on any of the pony's teeth, especially the wolf or canine teeth. Sometimes, if a pony has wolf teeth that are in the way of the bit, they are removed.

> **Some people may say:**
> **The bit needs to be held in place with enough pressure to give two wrinkles when in the corners of your pony's mouth.**
> This is because historically when many hundreds of soldiers were being trained a soldier made a mistake putting the bit too low in his horse's mouth. The bit became hooked over the horse's teeth causing it to rear. The General in charge at the time decided that all cavalry horses should carry the bit high enough to give two wrinkles in the corners of their mouths so this would not happen again.

Some people still follow this rule. The only rule to follow is to make sure your pony is comfortable. If the bit is too high it is uncomfortable! If the bit is too low it is dangerous!
If you ride your pony when he is tense he will develop incorrect muscles. He may become sore and he will find moving correctly difficult. He will lean and pull on the bit and you will feel this pull on the rein.

The reins

When you are riding your pony you will communicate with him, first by your intention, then your body language, then your rein. As your pony listens more to your body language you will need the reins less and less.
Before you ride it is important to understand how to use the reins correctly. By preparing your pony on the ground to follow the feel of his halter and line, you have prepared him to follow the feel of the rein. When the pony follows the feel of a rein it is called a rein aid.
When you used a feel of steady pressure to ask your pony to move on the ground, you were developing an understanding of how to use the rein to communicate with your pony.
Using this 'feel' will tell you how much pressure you need to ask your pony to respond to your rein aid.
Your pony must be able to feel through the rein what you are asking him to do so he can make the correct response.

If your reins are too long he will not be able to feel your contact easily.

Too short   **Too long**   **Correct length**

If they are too short, you may put too much pressure on the rein. This will make it difficult for you to ask him to relax and to turn.

When you use the reins it is important you do not use them to balance yourself or to hold onto because you are nervous or afraid. Your pony must feel that he is allowed to move. As you practise and use your reins you will adjust the length so that you can effectively communicate with your pony.

When you take hold of the rein it should be light but secure, so that it does not slip through your hands.

think
like a pony
IN THE SADDLE

You should wrap your fingers around the rein and secure it gently with your thumb.

When you ride you will hold the reins like this, with your hands and arm in a straight line, knuckles facing forwards and arms relaxed hanging by your side. In this position you can have a **shared** contact with your pony's mouth.

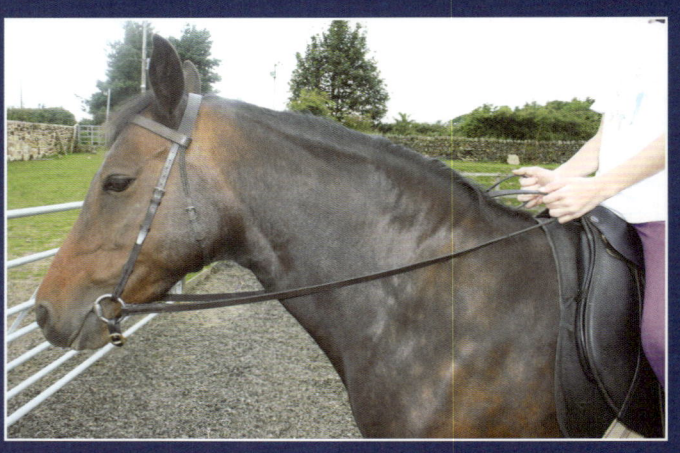

This contact should feel light and must allow your pony to move forward. The contact will give you feedback and make you aware of what your pony is doing. Holding the rein and having a contact with your pony is like holding his 'hand'.

Holding a friend's hand is reassuring and friendly but not restricting. You do not own your friend's hand, you share a contact with each other. You have to develop a use of both hands equally, to develop an even contact left and right.

To communicate with your pony your reins need to be about the same length as his neck. He needs to be free to move his neck as he walks, trots and later canters.

You may need to experiment with the length of rein you require to maintain a contact without pulling or restricting. You should think of having a clear straight line of communication between you and your pony.

Think Like a Pony, what does it feel like to share a contact?

Try this! Sharing a contact

With a partner stand facing each other.
Offer each other your hand to 'shake' as if you were greeting each other.

Notice how they take hold of your hand.
Is their feel too firm, too loose or just right?
Is this feel and contact reassuring?

Does it feel as if they have committed and want to hold you hand?

Find a feel and contact that you both like. Ask your partner to follow the feel of your hand. Do they follow willingly? Can you move freely together?

When you are riding, if you could reach your pony's mouth with your hands, you could politely guide him and direct him where you want to go. The reins are just like an extension of your hand.

Chapter 4
Learning to use the reins

You can use your reins with your body language to:
- Steer • Stop • Back up

Remember, when you hold your reins it should be like holding a friend's hand. To help you imagine what this feels like when you are holding the rein, pretend you are holding a duckling. You should hold the duckling so that you want him to be able to see where he is going. Hold him firm enough to stop him escaping but not so tight that you hurt him.

Riding will be more fun for you and your pony if you think about how to use the reins.

Try this! How much pressure do I use?

With a partner:

You are the rider and your partner is the pony.
Stand facing your 'pony partner' with your body balanced over your feet. Think of a smile across your chest and allow your shoulder blades to 'melt' down your back. This will allow you to stand up straight and tall without tension.

1. Close your fingers around your partner's index fingers as if you are holding the rein. Feel that you can hold them there without squeezing, but at the same time firm enough so that they are secure. Think of the duckling.

   Notice how this feels in your hand and arm.
   Ask your partner for feedback.

2. Now slowly start to increase the pressure from your hand. As you do so you will start to use muscles in your lower arm. Try to isolate the feel of using the muscles in your hand and your lower arm to put pressure on your partner's fingers.

Notice how this feels.

Ask your partner how this feels on their fingers.
Release the pressure. Practise putting pressure on your partner's fingers first with the muscles in your hand, then lower arm. Release the pressure without letting go of your partner's fingers. How would it feel if your partner never released the pressure on your fingers? If you never released the pressure on your partner's fingers they may feel uncomfortable and their hand and arm may become tense.

Think Like a Pony, if you never release the pressure on the rein, your pony would become tense and may even pull you.

3. Now use the muscle in your upper arm to put pressure on your partner's fingers.
Notice how this feels in your arm. Ask your partner how it feels.
When you use the muscles in your upper arm, your whole arm becomes stiff and your elbow moves backwards. Your partner will feel as if you are pulling them. Pressure from your whole arm is too much.

Think Like a Pony, your pony may feel as if you are pulling him backwards.
You will notice that it only takes a small amount of pressure to influence your partner's fingers. Pressure from your hand and lower arm is enough to communicate effectively.

4. Move your elbow behind your body. This will cause your partner to feel that they are being pulled.

Think Like a Pony who was moving forward. This would cause him to feel as if you are trying to stop him. This is a confusing signal.

What you have learned so far will help you to use the reins so that you can:
- Have a polite, shared contact on the rein.
- Learn how to hold the reins without pulling.
- Know how to release pressure to reward your pony.

When you have finished, swap over so you can both experience this.

Try this! Practising using the reins to communicate

Do this with a partner. You are the rider, your partner is the pony.

1. Sit facing each other. Both shuffle to the edge of your chair so that you are balanced and carrying your own weight. Put out your arms so that you just touch each other.

34

2. Your 'pony partner' holds the bridle by the bit (or if you are using a bitless bridle, the noseband). They can rest their hands on their legs if they want to and they should follow the feel of the bit.

You should take hold of the reins an arm's length from the bit, so that the reins are not slack.
Hold them as you have been shown. Stop the rein from slipping by lightly placing your thumb on top. Keep your wrist straight and relaxed, your elbow soft.
Do not press hard or your hand and arm will become tense.

3. Both partners must relax their shoulders and bend their arm at the elbow. Let your elbow hang by the side of your body and your forearm held out in front of you.

If your reins are too slack your partner will not feel your contact.

think *like a pony*
IN THE SADDLE

4. Can your partner feel your contact on the rein? Does it feel like you are holding their hand? Are they comfortable with this feel?

5. Now slowly increase the feel of steady pressure on the reins, so that your partner can feel it as they hold the bit. Try to use only the muscles in your hand.

How much pressure did you need?

36

6. Now increase your pressure on the reins using the muscles in your lower arm but do not move your arms forward. Imagine that you want the reins and bit to come towards you. If you pull and use the muscles in your upper arm or move your arm back you may cause your partner to pull back or become unbalanced.

Use the muscles in your hands and forearm to slowly increase the feel of pressure on the reins.

Did your partner feel this clear communication on the bit? If you rush then your partner may feel that you are pulling them.

think
like a pony
IN THE SADDLE

Think Like a Pony, this could be a confusing signal to your pony.

7. Now use the muscles in your upper arm and then take your arms behind your body. What happened to your partner? Did you unbalance them?

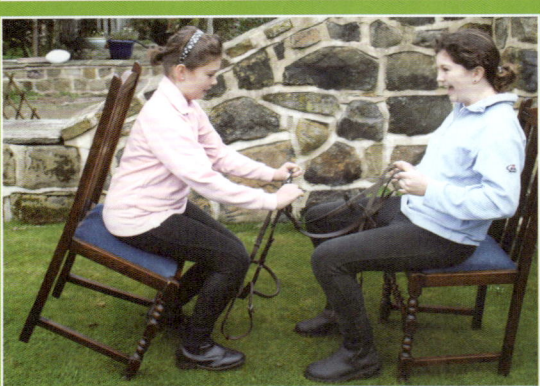

When you ride, if you take your elbows behind your body, you will be pulling your pony and restricting their movement.

Practise releasing the feel of pressure on the reins. Keep hold of the reins and try to release your hold by relaxing your hand just enough to release your pressure.

If you just drop the reins your partner will feel as if you have just let go of them. You are no longer holding their hand and your line of communication is broken.

Think Like a Pony, your pony will feel as if you have dropped them if you just abandon the rein and break your line of communication.

With your partner practise:
- **Increasing the pressure on the rein.**
- **Releasing the pressure on the rein.**

8. Lift the left rein up and out a little showing your partner the direction that you want them to go. See how little pressure it takes to influence and move the bit or bridle for your partner to feel it.

This is like directing your pony to turn left. Repeat this with your right rein.

9. Flex your wrists inward, like the girl in the picture, and ask your partner to follow your feel on the rein, first turning left then turning right.

think
like a pony
IN THE SADDLE

10. Now hold your wrists as if you were holding a trolley and ask them to follow your feel on the rein, to turn left, then turn right.

Were your signals as clear with your hands in this position?
You must use your reins separately: your left rein to direct and turn your pony left; your right rein to direct and turn your pony right.
Practise until you 'feel' you understand how to use the reins.

Make sure you feel what it is like to be the rider and the pony.
If you pull or restrict your pony with two reins, you may cause him to become nervous and afraid of your contact. When your pony is nervous, tense or upset he will show it in his body language.

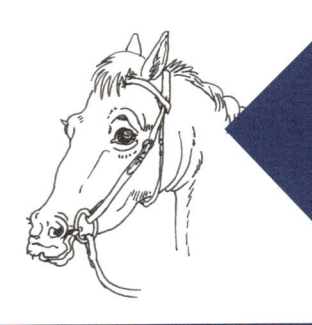

If he is in any way unsure about what you are asking or how you are asking it, your pony will look tense around his head and mouth. He may hold his jaw and mouth tight, as if he were chewing a lemon.

He may try to open his mouth, like a cross alligator.

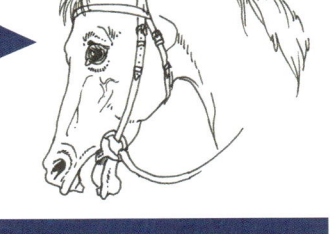

He may cross his jaw or mess with his bit like a child chewing on a toffee.

If your pony shows any of these signs when you are using the reins to communicate make sure:

- Your bit and bridle are the correct size and fit.
- Your reins and hands allow your pony to move.
- You are using your reins independently.
- You are not pulling on two reins.
- Your reins are not too short.
- You are not using your reins to balance yourself.

If you are consistent your pony will be able to make sense of what you are asking him and you will gain his trust and confidence.

REMEMBER to gain your pony's trust and confidence in your feel on the reins, you must learn to use them correctly.

Chapter 5
Where is your weight?

Ponies are strong and because of this you may think that they can easily carry you and the saddle.

True, they are strong, but you can make a pony weak by:
- Asking them to wear a saddle which does not fit.
- Not understanding how they need to move.
- Riding them incorrectly.
- Allowing their feet to become unbalanced.

Think like a pony…
- What does it feel like when you carry someone?
- What does it feel like when they move?
- Are they heavy?
- Do they affect your balance?
- Do you trust this person on your back?

Even if you are little or a light weight, when your weight is on your pony's back it will influence where he puts his weight! This is one of the most important things to consider before you ride your pony.

Try this! Where is your weight?

With a partner, one of you will be the rider and one the pony.

Ask your 'pony partner' to give you a piggy back. When you are comfortable and safe hold your partner like the girl in the picture.
In this position:

1. Sit up, 'think light' and carry your own weight.
    Ask your partner to walk forward.

2. Keeping hold of your partner 'think heavy' and sit back and down. Ask your partner to walk forward.

Is it easier for your partner to move when you are light or heavy?

3. Sit to the left and ask your partner to walk forward.

4. Sit to the right and ask your partner to walk forward.
   Could your partner walk straight?

5. Sit in the middle of your partner's back and carry your own weight.
   Ask your partner to start walking forward.
   When they are walking, shift your weight left or right and try to influence where they go.

Be careful, you don't want to unbalance them too much.

Did you influence the direction your partner walked by shifting your weight? Where would you need to put your weight if you wanted them to go forward, or backward?

6. Sit heavily to the left then ask your partner to try to pick up their left leg.

7. Sit heavily to the right then ask your partner to try to pick up their right leg.

Your partner cannot pick up their leg when you have your weight on it. For them to pick up their leg you first have to take your weight off it!

Think Like a Pony, your weight affects your pony as he lifts up his legs.

think
like a pony
IN THE SADDLE

8. Sit in the middle of your partner's back and carry your own weight. Ask your partner to move forward in a straight line.
Put your head and neck as far to the left and then to the right as far as you can without leaning.

How did moving your head affect their balance?

Think Like a Pony, your head is very heavy. When it moves it affects your balance and your pony's balance.

Talk to your partner and ask them what it was like to be your pony.
Where and how did they prefer you to sit so they could move easily?
Try to find someone small enough for you to carry on your back and this time you be the pony.

It is easier for a pony to move when the rider is light and balanced in the middle of his back.

45

think like a pony
IN THE SADDLE

Try this! Carry your weight

1.

1. Stand with your partner as shown in the photograph.

   You are going to be the pony and your partner is going to be the rider.

   Stand with your arm ready to support the 'rider'. Your arm is acting like the pony's back.

   Ask your 'pony partner' to place their arm on top of yours and flex their knees a little as if they were riding.

   - You will feel their weight on your arm.

2.

2. Now ask them to take one leg forwards and notice the increase in weight on your arm as you try to support them.

   Then ask them to take both legs forward.

   - Does it feel like they need more support?
   - Has the weight on your arm increased?
   - Do you feel as if your partner is pulling you forward or off balance?

3. What would happen to your partner if you were to take away your arm?
Because they are unbalanced, they cannot support themselves and they will fall over.

To reduce the weight on your arm, your partner must stand balanced, carrying their own weight over the balls of their feet.

Think Like a Pony, this is the position you need when you sit on your pony so that you are light and can support your own weight.
When you have felt what it is like to be the pony, swap over and repeat, this time being the rider.

You are going to learn to use this point of balance when you ride. When you put your foot in the stirrup you will think of balancing your body first on your bottom then over your feet.
To remind yourself where your point of balance is, stand with your arms by your side. Rock your weight forward into your toes and then backwards into your heels. Notice what happens to your body. To balance yourself you need to balance your weight over the balls of your feet.

think like a pony
IN THE SADDLE

When you sit in the saddle you must still think about balancing the weight of your body over the balls of your feet. Think that your ears are over your shoulders, shoulders are over your hips and your hips are over your feet. This will help you to sit light and in balance.

Sitting with your weight balanced over your feet, if your pony disappeared, you would land standing up on the floor.

Sitting with your weight too far forward, if your pony disappeared you would fall on your back.

Sitting with your feet too far back, if your pony disappeared you would fall on your face.

If you are unbalanced you are letting your pony carry all of your weight. This makes you heavy and may cause your pony's back to become tight and sore. He may be unwilling to go forward in walk, trot or canter. He may even refuse to jump.

Sitting with your feet and legs too far forward or too far back means treating your pony like a chair and expecting him to carry you.

It is essential that your pony feels that he can move when you sit on him. Learning to use your weight and body language correctly when you are riding is the first thing that you must do so that you can **ride naturally and in harmony with your pony.**

Being aware of your weight

A pony needs to shift his weight in order to be able to move each foot. You do this naturally when you are walking. You shift your weight without thinking so that you can lift one foot off the floor and then the other. When you ride a pony you have to learn to shift your weight, so that your pony can shift his weight and so you can move together.

It is like moving with your pony as your partner. Think of your feet as your pony's feet!

When you are riding and you want to change direction the best way to influence your pony is to look up and into the direction you want to step. This helps you to shift your weight.

When you ride your pony, to ride in harmony together, you shift your weight together. To prepare yourself to feel this when you ride, try the following.

Try this! Shifting your weight

1. **Stand with your legs hip width apart. Imagine you are standing in the middle of a clock face with 12 o'clock in front of you. Look straight ahead, your eyes level with the horizon. You should feel balanced.**

2. **Turn your eyes, nose, shoulders and belly button to point and look over your right hand to 1 o'clock.**

   Where is your weight now?

   Which leg can you move?

   Your weight should feel even in both legs.

think like a pony
IN THE SADDLE

3. Keep looking over your hand towards 1 o'clock. This time look up above the horizon.

Where is your weight now?

Which leg can you move?

Your weight should be in your left leg and you can pick up your right leg. If you cannot feel this lift your hand a little higher and look up.

4. Keep looking over you hand to 1 o'clock. This time look and point down towards the floor.

Where is your weight?

Which leg can you move?

Your weight should be in your right leg and you can pick up your left leg.

If you look down when you are riding and ask your pony to move a front leg, he may find it difficult, if you have your weight on that leg.

If you look up in the direction you are going, you will keep your weight in the correct place for your pony to do what you are asking.

never going to happen!

50

Chapter 6
Putting on the saddle

Your pony must be confident and accepting of the saddle before you ride him. You may understand what a saddle is but try to **'Think like a pony'**. To him, a saddle could be a wild beast or a strange object that may hurt him or cause him pain.

Make sure that your pony is clean and you have brushed him. Check there is nothing that can irritate him, especially where the saddle, girth or bridle will go.

Brushing your pony is another way to bond with him and check that he is OK. Make sure that you maintain a safe position when you are grooming him and are aware of his body language at all times.

Brush firmly with rhythm so it feels 'like a massage'. Watch to see if your pony is enjoying the experience. The expression on this pony's face shows the handler that the pony is having a good time.

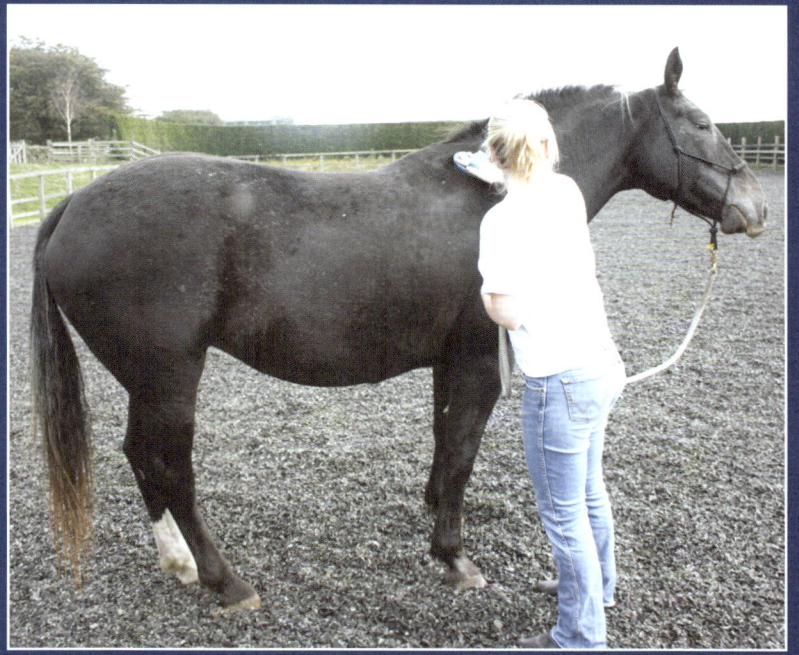

think *like a pony*
IN THE SADDLE

Exercise 1. Putting on the saddle

When you put the saddle on your pony's back it should be done sensitively and with consideration. You may be in a rush but your pony is not.
With adult supervision, in a safe place where you both feel comfortable, with the halter on and the lead rope attached.

1. Place the rope over your arm, or ask a parent or guardian to hold your pony.
   Pick up the saddle cloth and allow your pony to sniff it.

2. When he has sniffed it, rub him with it on his shoulder.

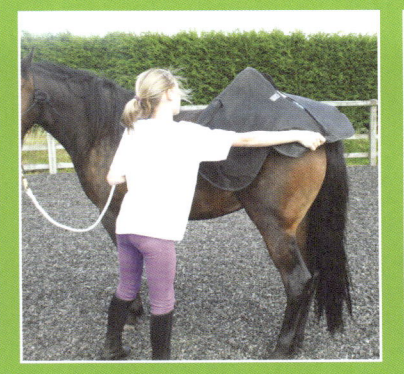

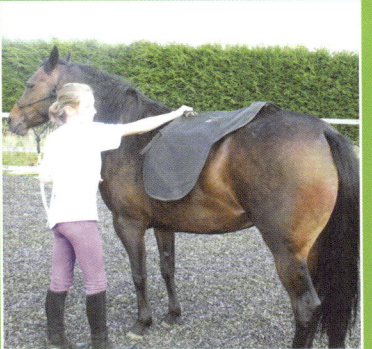

3. With a swinging action throw the saddle cloth over your pony's withers and stroke it down his back. Slide it over his hindquarters to make sure that your pony is comfortable with items around his body. This is essential preparation for riding. Place the saddle cloth on his back. Repeat this from both sides. If your pony appears worried or concerned repeat this until he relaxes.

If your pony moves his feet, be aware of his body language. Is he moving because:
- he is afraid,
- unsure,
- or trying to be the leader?

If he is afraid or unsure, slow down. If he is trying to be the leader, ask him to back up and stand still.
REMEMBER to use approach and retreat to build up your pony's confidence.

4. Place the saddle cloth over your pony's back towards the withers. If you need to use any other pads underneath to balance your saddle, put these on next.

5. Take hold of the saddle with two hands as shown in the picture. Make sure that your stirrups are run up and your girth is secure.

Allow your pony to sniff his saddle. This way he becomes familiar with it and can more easily accept it.

6. With a swinging action, gently place the saddle over your pony's back towards his withers, so it sits on top of the saddle cloth.

Check there is enough space for him to be able to move his shoulder and the saddle is supported by his rib cage.

7. When you are happy that the saddle is in the correct place let down the girth.

think like a pony IN THE SADDLE

Move around your pony in front of his head so he can see you. Make sure that you take your rope with you when you swap sides.

8. Standing parallel to your pony, reach under his tummy for the girth and lift it against his tummy so he can feel it. Fasten it just tight enough to stop the saddle slipping when he moves. Check the saddle's position and balance.

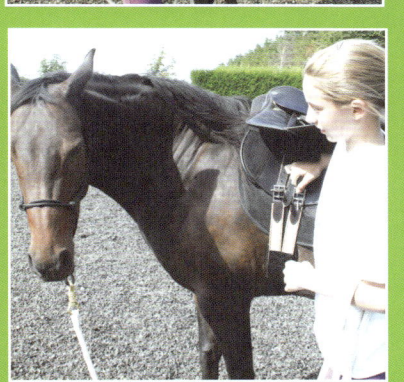

Be aware of his body language, watch for warning signals that he may be unsure or uncomfortable. Be ready to approach and retreat at any time to build his confidence.

Make sure you do not over-tighten the girth or tighten it too quickly. 'Think like a pony', how would you feel if someone fastened a belt around your waist? You would like it done slowly with consideration, allowing you time to adjust yourself and accept it.

If your pony reacts to the girth, try rubbing his tummy with your hand.

Lift the girth up and down against his belly a few times to give him time to get used to the feel. Take your time.

REMEMBER you are building his trust and showing him you are not acting like a predator. To build his trust you must be patient. A predator would move quickly.

If your pony acts dangerously or scared, his saddle may be causing him pain. Seek professional advice.

Try to saddle your pony from the left one day, the right the next, so that he gets used to you approaching him with the saddle from both sides.

When you have fastened the girth tight enough to allow your pony to move without the saddle slipping, you are going to ask him to move. This gives him time to relax and get used to the feeling of the saddle on his back and prepares him for riding.

9. Ask him to walk. He does not need to move very far, just enough to relax and get used to the feel of the saddle.

10. When he has moved a little in walk, ask him to stop. Give him a rub and be aware of his body language. Tighten the girth a little more. Check the position and balance of your saddle.

Now you can ask your pony to trot and if you want to ask him over an obstacle.

When he has moved in trot for just a little bit, stop him and see if his girth needs to be tighter. When you tighten the girth make sure you adjust it evenly from both sides so that the pressure feels even to your pony. If the girth will easily tighten you may need to ask your pony to move a little more and check the girth one more time.

Before you think of getting on you must always check that:
- The saddle has not slipped backwards or forwards.
- The saddle has not slipped to the left or to the right.
- The girth is not too loose or too tight. You should comfortably be able to slip your fingers between the girth and your pony's side.

11. Now let the stirrups down and ask him to move again.

When you are ready ask him to walk and trot.

This way he can feel the stirrups moving against his side. This prepares him for your moving legs.

12. If your pony appears frightened or scared move the stirrups against his side using approach and retreat to build his confidence.

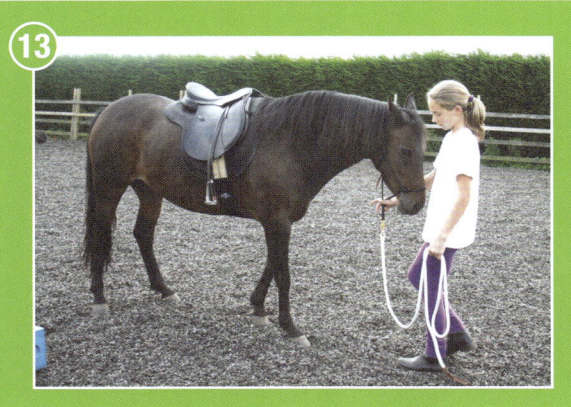

13. You can ask him forwards and backwards with the stirrups down.

When he is no longer afraid ask him to walk on again.

When he is confident try asking him to trot.

Always prepare your pony to ride this way then you will both be safe and be comfortable and have fun together.

think like a pony
IN THE SADDLE

Exercise 1a: Removing the saddle

When you are ready you can take the saddle off your pony's back.

1. Make sure that your rope is over your arm so that at any time you can take control of your pony. Check the fiador knot is in neutral. When you move from one side of your pony to the other always go around the front of your pony and take your rope with you.

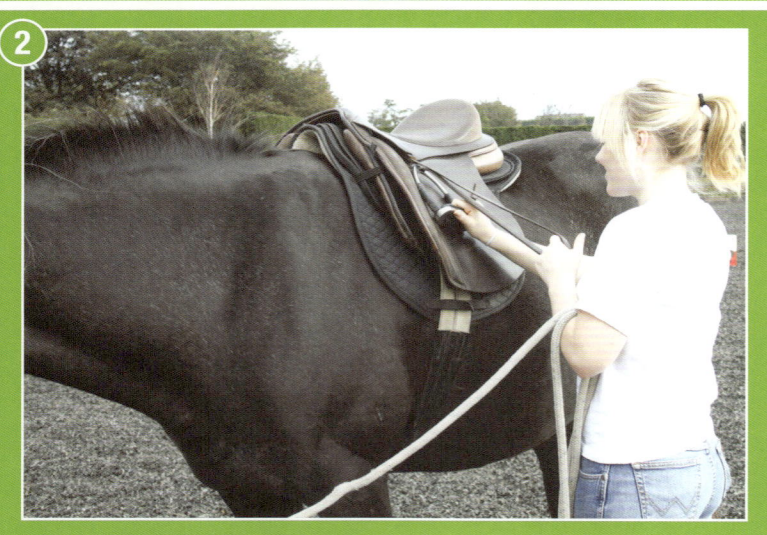

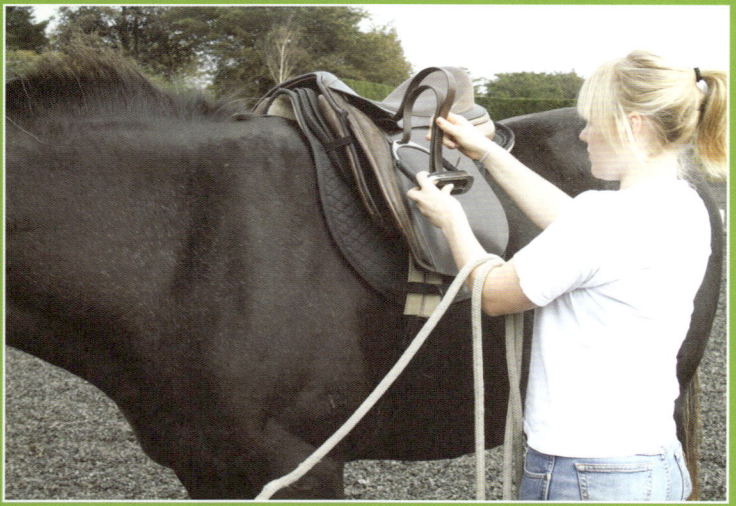

2. Run your stirrups up as shown in the photographs. Run the stirrup iron up the leather and thread the leather through the stirrup iron to secure it.

3. If your pony does not stand still, ask him to take a few steps back, relax and give him a friendly rub. **REMEMBER** you must be in control at all times.

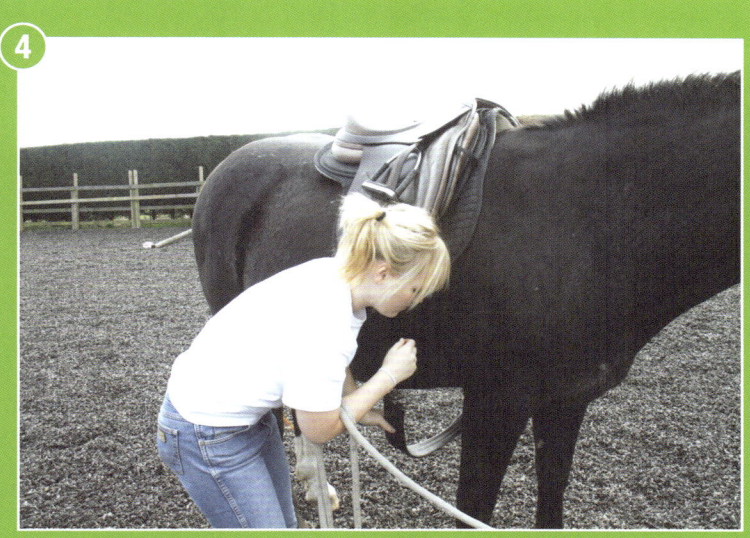

4. Now undo the girth completely and gently let it down to the floor. If at any time your pony moves, politely ask him to back up.

5. Thread your girth through your stirrup, like the girl in the picture.

think like a pony
IN THE SADDLE

6. Hold the saddle at the front and back, and lift it gently off towards you.

Watch his reactions and body language as you put the saddle on and take it off.

Is he happy with his saddle? If not, try to find out why.

If you get into the habit of looking at your pony's body, his muscle tone and posture, you will know if he is comfortable in his saddle.

Keep your saddle and girth and leathers clean and supple. Make sure that your saddle cloth is washed regularly and you always check the fit and balance of your saddle.

Your pony has to be comfortable and happy in his saddle when you ride him.

Chapter 7
Putting on the bridle

Preparation is everything and now you are prepared to confidently put the bridle on your pony.
- You have prepared him to follow your feel and lower his head so that he can relax.
- You have built his confidence in your touch so that you can help to make the experience pleasurable and safe for both of you.
- You now have an understanding of how to use the reins with feel to communicate with your pony.
- Your bridle and bit are the correct size and fit for your pony.

Exercise 2: Putting on the bridle

With adult supervision in a safe place where you both feel comfortable, with the halter on and the rope attached.

1. Hold the bridle in one hand and the reins in the other, as shown in the picture.

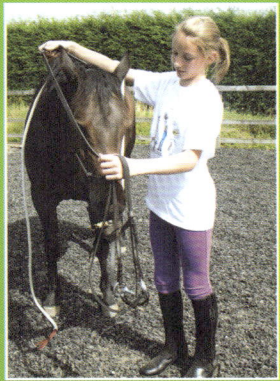

2. When your pony is relaxed and willing to, ask him to lower his head and place the reins over his head and neck.

Be confident, polite and be aware of his body language at all times. Be willing to use approach and retreat at any time. Your pony should by now be prepared to accept things around his head and trust you and your approach. If he reacts in a way which shows you he is not happy or he is afraid, it is up to you to gain his trust and confidence.

If he raises his head, stop and ask him to lower it. Be prepared to do this as many times as necessary.
REMEMBER to stay calm and relaxed and then he can relax.

3. When the reins are over his neck use pressure from the reins to ask your pony to lower his head and neck. When he does give him a rub.

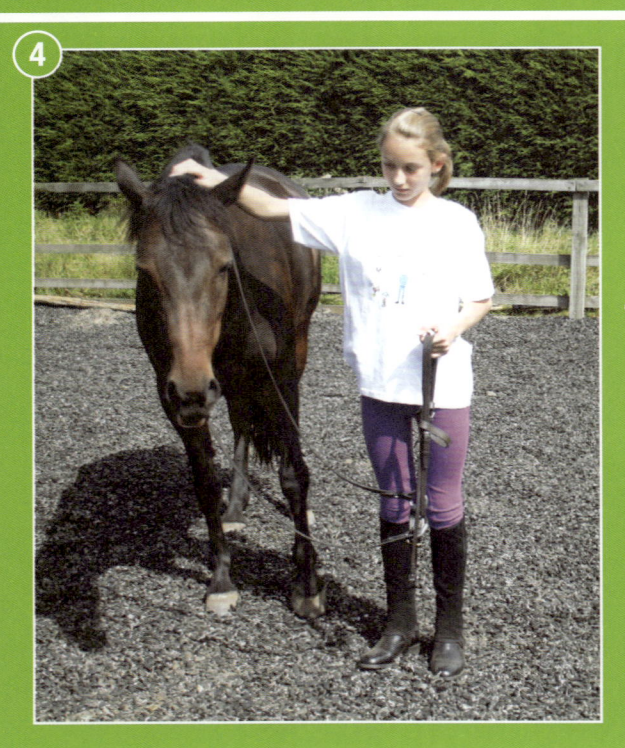

4. When he is relaxed undo the halter and take it off. Tie a safety knot in your halter and place it on the floor or hang it up.

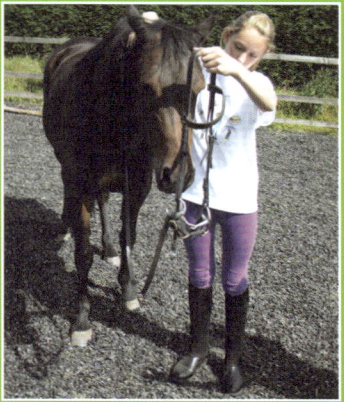

It does not matter how many times you ask your pony to lower his head and neck. What is important is that he can remain relaxed while you put on his bridle.

REMEMBER to make sure that you give your pony your attention, then he will give you his attention.

5. Still standing at the side of your pony with your right arm over your pony's neck and your left arm holding your bridle, offer the bridle towards your pony's head.

Take hold of the bridle now in your right hand by the headpiece and hold the bit in your left hand and offer it to your pony's lips.

Take your time. Let your pony think and 'feel' the experience.

Watch his body language for signs of tension.

Let him know that there is no rush by being patient, calm and remembering to smile.

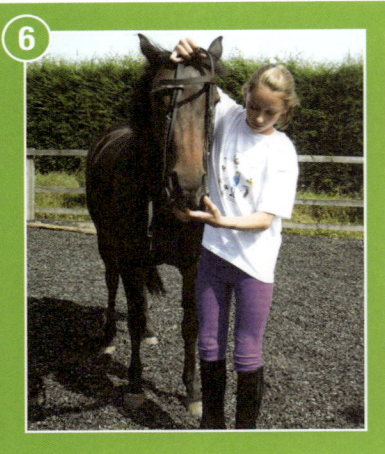

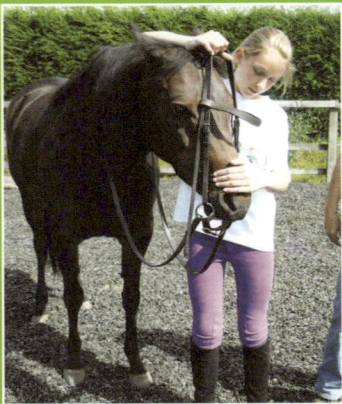

6. Use your hand gently to ask him to tip his nose to you.

Still holding the head stall in your right hand lift it up just a little to put a gentle feel on the bit.

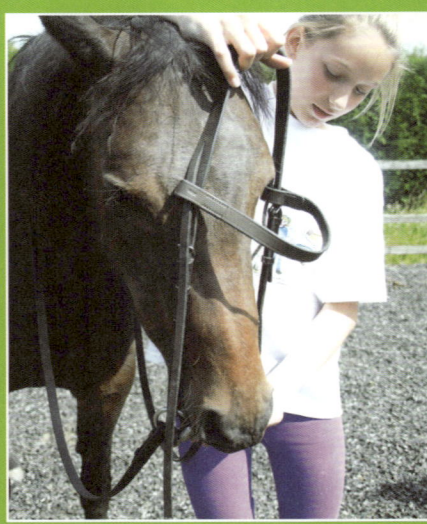

7. Gently lift the bit towards your pony's mouth as if you were asking him to 'taste it'.

At the same time keep a feel on the head stall, 'lifting' the bit into his mouth.

Be patient, making sure not to pull or push.

If he raises his head use steady gentle pressure from your arm over his head and neck to ask him to lower it again.

When your pony takes the bit in his lips you can encourage him with a gentle lift on the head stall, to take it into his mouth. Wait and give him time to accept this.

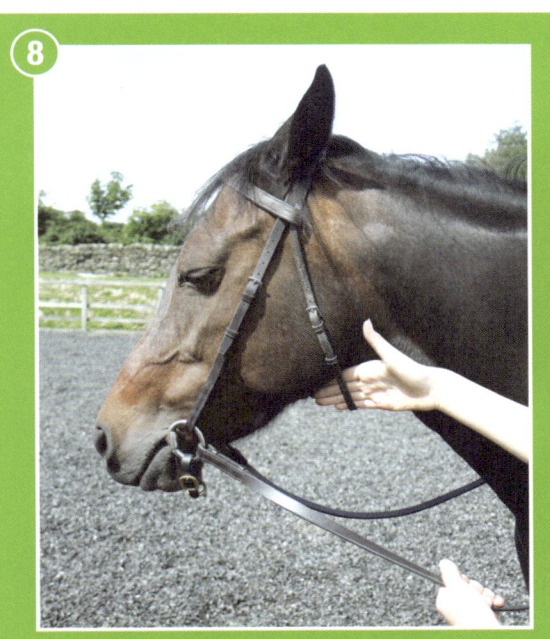

8. When he puts the bit in his mouth give him a gentle rub to say thank you and fasten the throatlash. Allow a hand's width between the jaw and the throatlash so that your pony can move his head. If the throatlash is too loose his bridle could come off.

9. Check your reins are the correct length. The buckle or middle of the rein should reach his wither. If they are too long you will find them difficult to handle. If they are too short your pony will not be able to use his neck.

If your pony acts dangerously or throws his head around violently seek professional advice.

If you are using a bitless bridle, use the same technique but instead of putting the bit in his mouth offer the noseband over his nose.

When you have successfully put on his bridle and checked everything is correct, give him a friendly rub to say thank you.

If you want to, you can put your bridle on over your halter. This way your parent or guardian can lead you while you are learning to ride.

Exercise 2a: Removing the bridle

When you are ready you can take your pony's bridle off.

1. Pick up you halter with the rope attached. Place the halter around his neck and tie it.

2. Undo the throatlash.

Place your hand on top of his browband near to his ears. Use a feel of steady pressure to ask him to lower his head so that you can slip his bridle over his ears and drop it forward and down.

You may need to put one hand on his nose to encourage him to drop his nose and relax. That's OK. Make sure that you take time and build up his confidence. Use approach and retreat at any time.

think *like a pony*
IN THE SADDLE

3. Now take the reins over his head and loop them through the throatlash and fasten it.

This will stop your reins getting tangled up and will make it easier to carry your bridle.

think *like a pony*
IN THE SADDLE

4. When you have successfully removed the bridle you can put on the halter.

REMEMBER you are always preparing your pony to respond to what you are asking him to do. If you need to build up his confidence in putting on and taking off his bridle think about asking him to lower his head and neck as often as possible. When he does, give him a friendly rub so that he enjoys the experience.

Chapter 8
Following the feel of the bridle

So that your pony is better prepared to ride, you can check that he understands how to respond to your rein aid before you ride him.

You should check from the ground that he can:
a) Flex left and right.
b) Lower his head.
c) Back up.
d) Lead forward.

Exercise 3: Asking your pony to flex to the left and right

With adult supervision in a safe place where you both feel comfortable with the bridle on:

1. Stand at the side of your pony by his shoulder; your feet facing towards his head.

   Place your hand nearest to your pony on his neck and hold the rein on that side with the other hand.

   Slide your hand down the rein towards his mouth. With a gentle feel on the rein imagine your pony is going to drop his nose a little and flex his neck just enough to look at you.

Keep your fingers light as you use a steady feel of pressure down the rein.

Think of a **lift** in the rein as you ask your pony to look towards you.

Start as gently as possible and increase the pressure until he responds. The moment he drops his nose a little and looks at you release your pressure and stop asking.

2. Give your pony a rub to reward him.

Be patient with yourself and experiment with your feel and the way you ask your pony to move his head and neck and respond to the rein.

REMEMBER you may have a piece of hard metal in a soft mouth, so go slow and have fun.

When you can successfully ask your pony to follow the feel on the rein to one side then repeat on the other side.

If he does not follow the feel of the rein equally to the left and to the right try to understand why.
- **Is he still stiffer on one side than the other?**
- **Does he trust you both sides?**
- **Are you pulling him around?**
- **Is your feel too heavy or too quick?**
- **Are you releasing your feel the minute he responds and flexes his head and neck?**
- **Relax him if necessary with massage on his head and neck.**
- **Are his teeth ok? If he tilts his head to follow the bridle he may need to see your equine dentist or vet.**

think like a pony
IN THE SADDLE

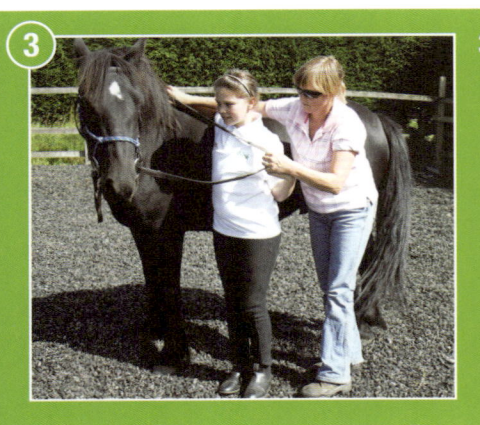

3. If your pony moves his feet when you ask him to flex towards you, allow him to move and keep asking him to flex. Make sure your feet stay parallel to his and move with him. The moment he tries to do what you are asking reward him by releasing the pressure. You may need your parent or guardian to help you with this.
If he still finds flexing in the bridle difficult, go back to asking him to flex in his halter and build up his confidence and your feel.

Exercise 3a: Asking your pony to lower his head

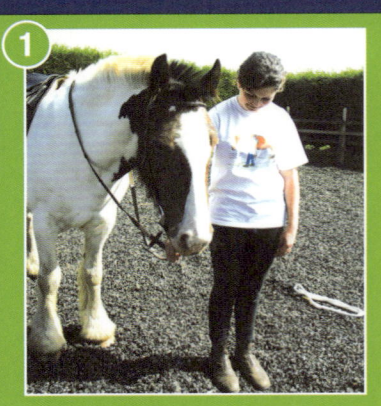

1. When he can confidently and easily flex left and right, ask him to lower his head. Stand at the side of your pony and hold both the reins in one hand. With a gentle downward feel on the reins slowly ask him to lower his head and neck forward and towards the ground.

This is important preparation for riding so take your time and make sure it is a pleasurable experience for you both.

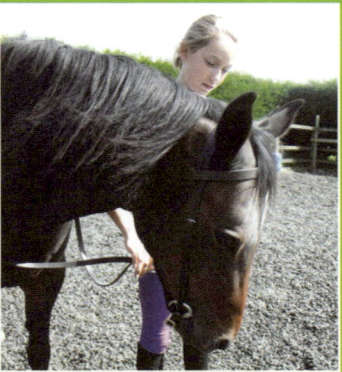

2. If your pony finds this difficult and resists, ask him to flex left then right then down.

You can help him to follow your feel by placing one hand over his neck to encourage him down as you have done before.

When you are riding you will learn to ask your pony to take a few steps backwards. You have asked him to step back in a halter but not in his bit or bridle. Preparing him from the ground will make it easier to ask him to step backwards when you ride.

REMEMBER **to back up, your pony must lower his head and neck so that he can lift his back. If he lifts his head his back will hollow and backing will be uncomfortable.**

Exercise 3b: Asking your pony for a few steps backwards

1. Stand in front of your pony. Hold the reins lightly where they attach to the bit or bridle and ask him to lower his head and neck.

   Check that your feel on the rein is NOT suggesting that your pony tips his nose to his chest. This would cause him to be tight in the jaw and he will not be able to relax. He may even open his mouth to avoid the bit.

2. When he has lowered his head and neck, have the intention that you want your pony to back up. Using the lightest pressure start to give a 'go backward' feel on the bit or bridle to suggest he move away from you.

3. If your pony does not respond, slowly increase the feel of backward pressure in **one** rein. Try to shift his weight into one leg as you have done before when you worked on the ground in his halter. The moment he responds, stop and reward him by releasing the pressure.

4. If he still does not respond, tap your foot to signal him to move backwards. Keep a backward feel on the bit or bridle. The moment he responds, stop and reward him. You could also ask your adult to tap him for you.

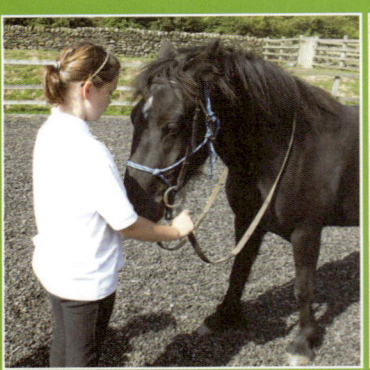

It is important not to increase the pressure on the bit or bridle too much or your pony may feel like you are pushing him and will push back on you!

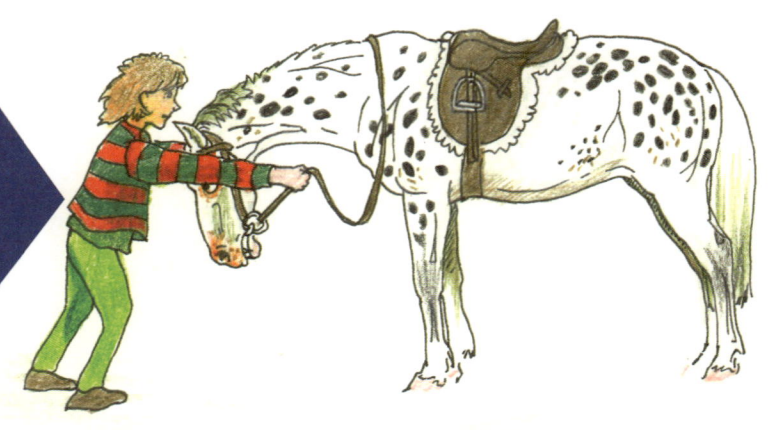

> If you increase the pressure too much or too quickly, your pony may try to raise his head and neck to avoid any uncomfortable feeling.

You want your pony to understand that a slight backward feel on the rein and bit means move backwards.

If at any time in the exercise your pony raises his head, use a feel on the reins and ask him to lower it.

If he finds stepping backwards difficult check:
- You are rewarding him for trying.
- You increase the pressure on one rein at a time to get in time with his feet.

Pressure from the left rein will move his left front foot and his right hind foot.
Pressure from the right rein will move his right front foot and his left hind foot.

REMEMBER your pony moves backwards in diagonal pairs.

If your pony finds moving backwards difficult in his bridle try to understand why.
- Are his teeth hurting?
- Is your feel too heavy?
- Are you pulling the bit or bridle down instead of giving a clear backward feel?

Keep practising until your pony can move backwards from a light pressure on the bit or bridle, without you having to signal to him.

If at any time your pony leans forward on the bit or bridle, or tries to walk forward:
- Put the reins in one hand and straighten your arm.
- Give him a firm rhythmical signal on his chest with your free hand or with your foot.

This will let him know this is not what you want.

Before you ride your pony he must understand that a gentle feel of backward pressure from the rein means 'move your weight, then your feet backwards'.

This is essential preparation to teach your pony to stop when you ride. Think that you are trying to resist your pony's forward movement!

When you can ask your pony to flex his head and neck and take a few steps backwards you are going to lead him forwards.

Exercise 3c: Leading your pony forward

1. **Stand by the side of his neck, your feet facing forward.**

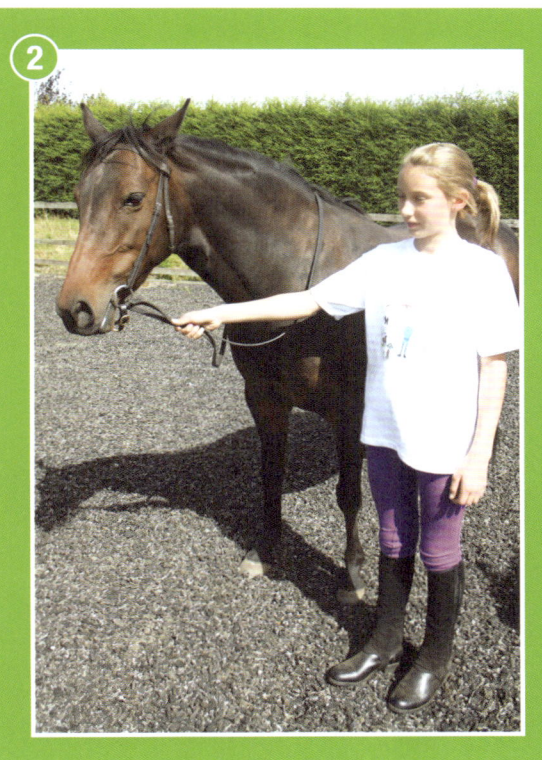

2. Holding both reins in one hand, use your intention and body language to show your pony that you want him to move forward. At the same time offer the reins forward.

3. If he does not walk forward with you, lift out your free arm as a signal to go forward. If he ignores this signal, tap behind you towards your pony's hindquarters. Be aware of his body language and try to understand why he is not walking forwards. Do not use the reins to pull him forward.

think
like a pony
IN THE SADDLE

4. If he does not respond to your arm signals, you may need to use a stick to extend your arm and make your signal clearer.

When he is walking forward, give him a rub and lead him around in a small circle.

5. When he has walked a small circle ask him to stop using your intention, body language and if necessary a backward feel on your rein to ask him to stop and back up.

78

If he does not want to stop, make the circle you are walking smaller making sure you remain at your pony's side. Make sure you are not in front of his feet then try stopping again, making sure you use your intention first, body language second. Smile and relax then give a backward feel on the rein.

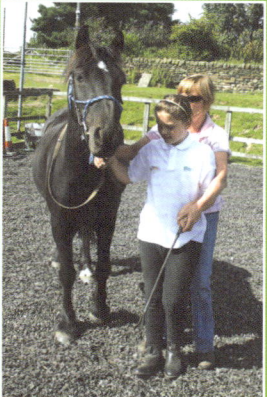

6. If he still does not stop, he may be ignoring your body language. Use a stick to make your signals clearer. If necessary tap in front of him to signal stop and back up.

If he still finds stopping difficult:
- Check your intention, body language and feel on the rein.
- Go back to working through the same exercises in his halter to build his respect, confidence and your leadership skills.

This is excellent preparation for riding so take your time and have fun.

When you can, ask your pony to:
- Flex
- Lower his head
- Backup
- Step forward
- Stop

You are prepared to ride.

think like a pony
IN THE SADDLE

Before you think of riding check that your pony:
- Is supple and flexible and relaxed.
- Is happy with his saddle and bridle.
- Has well-balanced feet.
- Has had his teeth checked.

Check that you:
- Are as supple and flexible as possible.
- Are dressed ready to ride.
- Are relaxed and calm.
- Are happy with the feel of your hat and boots.
- Your smile shows that you are happy, confident and ready to go.

Chapter 9
Getting on and off your pony

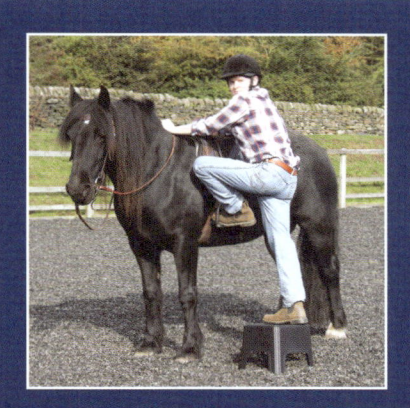

Practise mounting and dismounting from both sides to improve your co-ordination, balance and athleticism.

Try this: Mounting practice

1. Find a strong safe gate or a post and rail fence. Stand with your left side next to the gate. This is your imaginary 'pony'.

2. Hold the gate and look forward as if you are looking at your pony's head.

3. Put your right leg up on the gate as if you were putting your foot in the stirrup.

4. Now flex your knee and bounce 'to spring' up onto the gate. At the same time push down on the gate to help yourself up.

   It is important that you think of 'springing' up from the ground.

5. Stand balanced on the gate and turn your hip and belly button to face your 'pony's head'. From this position you could safely get down if you wanted to.

6. When you are balanced and ready, put your left leg over the gate. You are now on your pony!

Did you know?

The cavalry soldiers only ever mounted from the left side, so that they did not stab their horses with their swords!

You do not have to worry about carrying a sword, so are free to mount or dismount your pony which ever side you want to, if it is safe to do so.

This way you are preparing him to accept you on both sides and he will not be startled when you suddenly appear on his right side.

If you lead your pony through a gate or narrow gap in his tack make sure that you:
a) Run your stirrups up so that they do not get caught on anything.
b) Lead your pony from his shoulder so that you can accurately control his movements.
c) Hold the reins in one hand.

Exercise 4: Preparing your pony for you to mount

With adult supervision, in a safe place where you both feel comfortable, tack up your pony. Make sure you move him in his saddle and check his girth, tightening the girth in stages as you have done before.

1. Stand at your pony's left shoulder looking over his withers.
   Hold the reins in your left hand and rest your left hand on your pony's withers. Place your right hand on the front of your saddle.

   Now give your pony a firm rock from side to side to ask him to put his weight in all four feet. This way when you mount he will not have to move to rebalance himself.

Your pony must balance his weight on all four feet before you get on. If he is resting a foot or he is not balanced, he may need to move in order to balance himself when you try to mount.

2. When he has his weight evenly balanced jump up and down a little to let him know you are about to 'climb on up'.

3. If he moves, look at his body language to see if he is afraid or unsure or if he is trying to be the leader. If he is afraid or unsure move with him and keep hold of the reins. Keep jumping until he stops. When he stops, stop jumping and give him a rub, then start again. This way you are helping to build his confidence and trust in you.

Be prepared to use approach and retreat by making your jumps smaller then building them up as he becomes more confident.

If he is trying to be the leader use the reins to ask him to stop and back up.

4. When you can jump up and down a little in this position and your pony does not move, take hold of the stirrup in your right hand. With a gentle swinging action tap the stirrup against his side, as you have done before. Your pony should now be confident with you doing this.

When you have done steps 1-4 on his left side, repeat on his right side, holding the reins in your right hand.

REMEMBER it is important to prepare your pony from both sides so that he accepts you in both eyes.

When your pony can stand still and balanced he is ready for you to get on.

You should be able to mount your pony from the ground, from a mounting block or with help from someone else. Then you are prepared for any situation.

Exercise 4a: Getting on from the ground

If you feel at all unsure leave your halter on underneath your bridle and ask your helper to keep hold of the rope line.

1. Check your pony's weight is evenly balanced and he is ready for you to get on. Stand at your pony's left side, facing towards his head. Hold your reins and a chunk of mane in your left hand. Take hold of the front of the saddle in your right hand and prepare to pull yourself up by pulling on your pony's mane and pushing down on the saddle.

Pulling on his mane does not hurt your pony. If you pull on the back of the saddle it will cause the saddle to pull and twist on your pony's back. This will hurt him and can cause his back to become sore.

2. When you are ready, lift your left foot into the stirrup. With your right leg bounce a little to get yourself ready to spring and jump up.

think like a pony
IN THE SADDLE

3. As you jump up, pull on your pony's mane keeping your belly button facing forward between his ears. When you are up, stand in the stirrup as shown in the picture. Lean over the withers and stroke your pony with your right hand. In this position you can get down quickly if you need to.

**If your saddle has slipped, jump down and check your girth.
Check your saddle position.**

4. If your pony moves when you try to get on, step down.
   Ask him to take a few steps backwards.
   The moment he relaxes, try again to get on. Take your time to build his confidence and trust in you. Look at his body language to try and understand why he is moving, then you will know how to help him to relax.

   If he acts dangerously, seek professional advice.

5. When your pony can stand still, mount again, put your right leg over the saddle and gently sit down. Put your right foot in the stirrup. Keep hold of the reins in your left hand.

6. Now you are sitting on your pony, relax, breathe out and smile. Let him feel that you are happy, confident and relaxed. If you are nervous or tense he will sense it. Be determined to be a good leader who he can trust.

Give him a friendly rub on his withers.

86

Exercise 4b: Getting on from a mounting block or a safe object

Getting on from a safe object or mounting block may be more comfortable for you and your pony. From this position your pony can see you above him. You are now more likely to look like a predator, about to attack.

Before you use a mounting block make sure your pony is confident to stand next to the mounting block with you standing on it. Use the skills you have learned in **'Think like a Pony on the ground'** to:

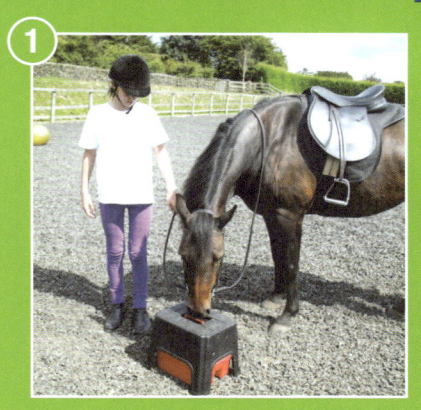

1. Ask you pony to stand near and sniff the mounting block.

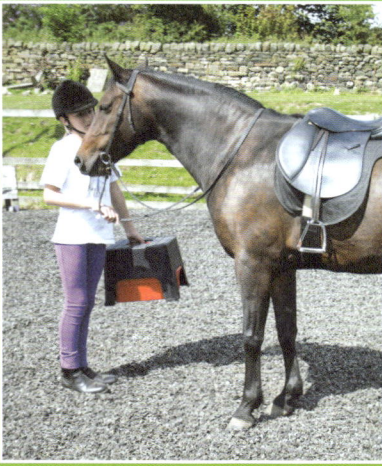

2. Move a mounting block around (if possible) so your pony can see it move and see it in both eyes. You can use approach and retreat to build his confidence. Allow him to move if he is afraid, or ask him to back up to control his feet if he is trying to take over.

You can stand on a mounting block and wait quietly giving him a scratch or a friendly hug. You can then get him used to standing still while you wave or move so that he is confident with you above him.

When you are confident that he feels safe and comfortable next to the mounting block, you can follow the instructions for getting on.

Exercise 4c: Getting on with a 'leg up'

Hold the reins, mane and the front of the saddle and rock your pony to put his weight in all four feet. Prepare to pull yourself up using the mane.

When you are ready, give your helper your leg like the girl in the picture. Bounce a little in time with each other. Then with assistance from your helper, count to three and spring up from the floor.

TO THE HELPER: Make sure you bend from your knees and you are secure and balanced. You are not throwing your child on their pony! You are acting as a springboard to help them up. If your pony moves, stop and ask him to back up.

Exercise 4d: Dismounting

Put both your hands on your pony's neck. Slip your feet out of the stirrups. Lean forward, just a little.
Now swing your right leg over your pony's back.
Dismount and hold your reins in one hand.
If your pony moves forward at any time, use your reins and ask him to stop and back up.
Take your time and have fun.
Make sure you practise getting on and off both sides.

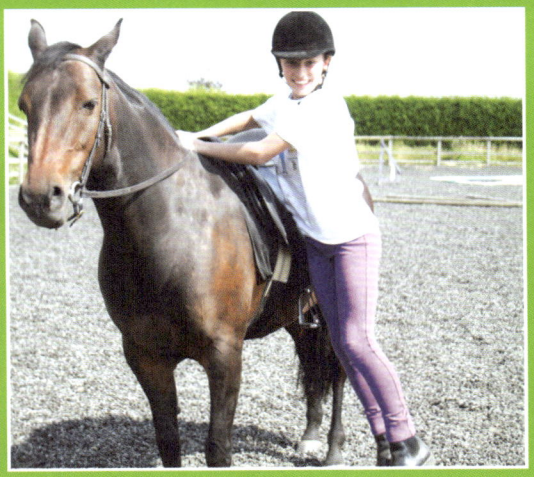

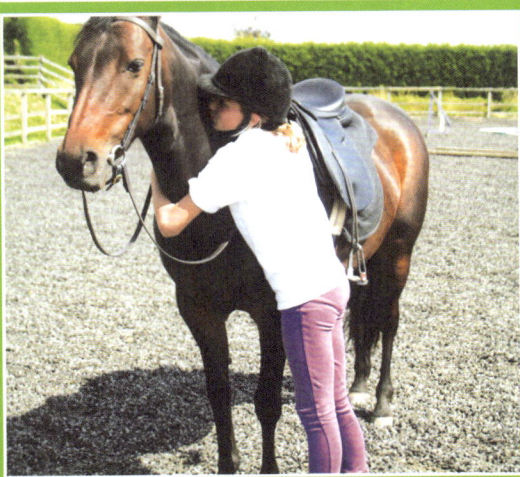

Chapter 10
Flexing

When you are riding you want to be a good leader for your pony. This means that you must be in control of where you both go, when you go and how you get there! Then you and your pony can stay safe and have fun together.

The first thing to do when you sit on your pony is to make sure that he is relaxed and listening to you. If he is tense or alert he will be ignoring you and you will find it difficult to communicate with him.

One of the best ways to ask your pony to relax is by first checking that you are relaxed, then you can ask him to flex his head and neck around to you. When he does you can give him a friendly rub to say thank you.
Flexing not only relaxes your pony but prepares him if you need to use an emergency stop.

It is like checking your brakes. You would not get into a car or ride your bike if your brakes did not work. It can be frustrating or frightening if your pony thinks that he is in control, even more frightening if he does not stop when you want him to.

If you are afraid you might start to pull on both the reins to try to control your pony. Pulling on two reins will only lead to more resistance and tension between you both and may cause your pony to straighten his head and neck and pull against you. Pulling on two reins can even cause a pony to panic and run faster!

If your pony does not stop when you ask him to you must have a plan to take control without panicking. This means you must be prepared.
Your pony can only pull you if:
- **His head and neck are straight.**
- **You pull with two reins to stop him.**

Try this: Using one rein to stop

Your partner is the 'pony' and must take the rope line and hold it firmly in two hands as shown in the picture. This will be the bridle. They must keep hold of the rope like this. You are the handler. Hold the ends of the rope lines, these are the reins.

Ask your pony to walk on and walk behind them. When you are ready ask them to trot and run behind them. Ask your 'pony' to pull and try and run away from you. Try to stop them by pulling back with both reins.
You will just end up pulling each other.

think like a pony
IN THE SADDLE

Think Like a Pony. If you try to pull on two reins to stop your pony, he will just pull harder because he is stronger than you!

Ask your 'pony' to walk on, then trot again. When you are ready ask them to try to pull and run away, this time keep hold of one end of the rope and let go of the other! Your partner must keep hold of the rope with two hands.

If you get this right they will turn to face you. When they turn and face you, you have caused them to turn (flex) and STOP.

They cannot pull you anymore if you only use one rein to stop them.

You will learn to use one rein to stop your pony, so that he does not learn to pull you.

To prepare your pony to stop with one rein you must make sure that his head and neck are flexible by asking him to flex left and right every time you ride.

If your pony can set his head and neck straight then he can pull you.

If his head and neck are flexed and bent then he cannot pull.

Exercise 5: Using the reins to ask your pony to flex

With adult supervision, in a safe place where you both feel comfortable, tack up your pony and prepare to ride.

1. When you are ready, mount your pony and pick up the reins, holding them in front of the saddle. Check they are about the same length as your pony's neck.

Close your fingers gently around the reins and put your thumb on top. Relax your shoulders and bend your arm at the elbow. Let your arm hang by the side of your body and your forearm held out in front of the saddle. Try to sit in balance by thinking that your ears are over your shoulders, your shoulders are over your hips, your hips are over your feet and your feet are underneath your body.

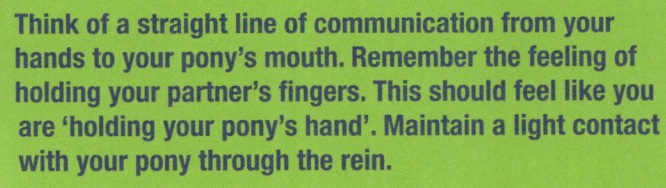

Think of a straight line of communication from your hands to your pony's mouth. Remember the feeling of holding your partner's fingers. This should feel like you are 'holding your pony's hand'. Maintain a light contact with your pony through the rein.

2. You are going to use your left rein to ask your pony to flex to the left.

With a steady feel lift your left rein up and out, away from your pony's neck just enough to ask him to move his head. Think that you would like him to drop his nose and look around towards you. A slight lift in the rein will communicate this to your pony.

Be careful not to ask quickly, or use too much pressure. This may cause him to resist or move his feet.

If you want him to be soft, you must be soft.

Use your fingers lightly and close your hands slowly, so you do not pull.

When he has flexed, show him he has done the right thing by putting your reins back into neutral and give him a friendly rub or stroke.

If your pony moves when you ask him to flex, he may be confused and think that he has to follow the feel of the rein and move his feet. He may walk around in a circle for a long time trying to work out what is happening.

If he keeps moving put your hand on his neck in front of the withers to help you to balance while you are asking him to flex. Make sure that you are relaxed in the saddle and that your legs are not asking your pony to go. Check you are not leaning and causing him to be unbalanced.

This girl is leaning and causing her pony to become unbalanced. She is taking the rein too far away from her pony's neck to try and pull him.

Think that your feet can reach towards the ground and imagine that you can drop an anchor from the ball of your foot. This will help you to be 'anchored' and still be in the saddle.

The moment he can stand still with some flexion release your feel on the rein and put the rein back into the neutral position. Give your pony a rub to show him he has done the right thing.

think like a pony
IN THE SADDLE

When he has successfully flexed to the left, use the right rein to ask him to flex to the right.

Ask your pony to flex around and look towards you two or three times on both sides. Take your time and build his confidence until he can look towards your leg.

This way if your pony frightens you by pulling or running away you can:
- Put one hand on the mane to keep you balanced and secure.
- Drop an anchor from your feet.
- Have the intention you want to stop.
- Use one rein to ask him to stop.
- Use one rein to ask him to flex left or right all the way around towards your leg until he stops. This way he cannot go anywhere.

96

Practise this on your pony so if an emergency happened you would know what to do.

If you want to you can practise this with your halter under your bridle whilst your handler holds the rope until you feel confident and safe.

The more you practise flexing your pony left and right the more willing your pony will be to follow your light feel on the rein.

Chapter 11
Sitting in balance

The way that you sit in the saddle and where you put your weight will influence your pony's movements.

This is your body language.

A pony can feel very small changes in your body language. Becoming aware of your intention, thought and body language is an essential part of communicating with your pony.

Your pony will not be able to move freely if you are not sitting in balance because you will feel like a heavy weight that he finds difficult to move. By learning how to move with your pony and staying in balance with him will help you to move freely together.

When your pony is not responding as you want him to, the first thing that you should check is your intention and body language. How do you influence your pony with your body language?

Try this: Feeling your seat bones

1. Sit on a chair. Sit upright, tall and relaxed with your feet on the floor.

   Place your hands under your bottom so that you can feel your seat bones.

2. Rock forwards and backwards.

3. Slump in the chair.

4. Arch your back.

When you move you can feel the weight change through your seat bones on your hands.

Think Like a Pony, when you are riding poke your seat bones into your pony's back and he will object. He may shrink away from your pointy bottom!

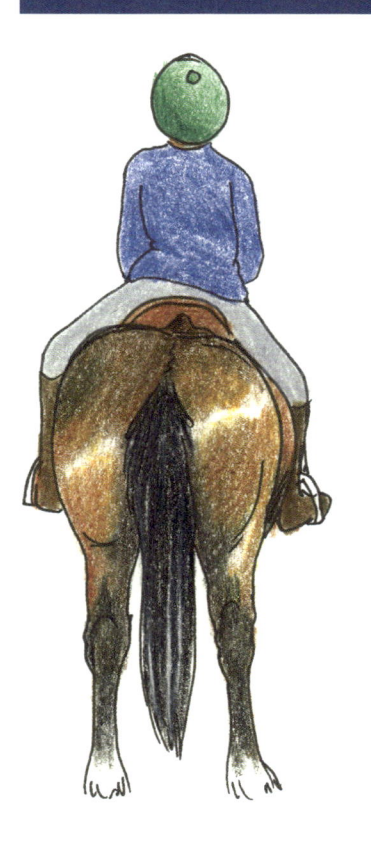

Your pony can feel your seat bones, even through his saddle. He can especially feel if you sit crookedly or to one side. If you are crooked you will be heavier on one side and you will cause your pony to follow your weight and he will become crooked.

think like a pony
IN THE SADDLE

Try this: Using your intention and body language

You are going to be the rider and your partner is going to be the pony.

Ask your 'pony partner' to sit on a chair with their feet on the floor. This way they are balanced and can support their own weight.

1. Sit on your partner's knees. Make sure your feet are flat on the floor.

- Imagine you can grow up tall.
- Your back and neck are soft and straight.
- As you breathe you can you lift up your ribcage.
- Imagine a smile across your chest and your shoulder blades sliding and melting down your back.
- Check you are looking straight ahead.
- Check your shoulders are over your hips and your hips are balanced over your seat bones.
- Relax your shoulders and bend your arm at the elbow. Let your elbows hang by the side of your body and your forearms held in front of you.
- Feel your feet on the floor.
- Breathe and smile!

Notice how this felt and ask your partner:
- Do you feel heavy or light?
- Are they comfortable?

2. Now arch your back and ask your partner:
- Do you feel heavy or light?
- Are they comfortable?

3. Now round your shoulders and back and ask your partner:
- Do you feel heavy or light?
- Are they comfortable?

Think Like a Pony, before you can ask your pony to move forward you must check that you are carrying your own weight as much as possible, so that you are light in the saddle.

The easiest way to do this is to imagine that your feet are on the ground. Your toes are pointing in the same direction as your pony's feet, you are balanced and your muscles are relaxed.

When you ride it is easier to direct your pony and influence his movement if your feet face forwards in the direction you and your pony are moving. Turning your toes out or in affects your seat bones and when you ride, your pony will feel this.
If you ride with your toes turned out, your thighs will not be in contact with the saddle and your bottom will be tight, this could cause your pony to stop moving.
If you ride with your toes turned in you will be gripping with your thighs and this will prevent you and your pony moving together.

Try this: Walking in balance

1. Walk forwards with your feet facing forward for about ten strides.

2. Now turn your toes in and try to walk another ten strides or so. Notice how this feels?

3. Walk forwards again with your feet facing forward then turn your toes out and try to walk. Notice how this feels?

When your toes are turned in or out you cannot move freely. Your balance may be affected and your muscles will become tight.

think *like a pony*
IN THE SADDLE

When you ride your pony in walk it feels like you are walking together. To feel this in the saddle you must be able to move as freely as you do when you walk on the ground.

When you are riding you should feel as if you could walk on the floor with your pony.

REMEMBER if at any time your pony was to disappear, you should be left standing on the floor.

think like a pony
IN THE SADDLE

Exercise 6: Sitting in balance on your pony

With adult supervision, in a safe place where you both feel comfortable, tack up your pony and prepare to ride. When you are ready mount your pony.

To get your leg in position, take your whole leg off your pony's side. Move your thigh under your bottom and then allow your leg to hang naturally.

When you place your foot in the stirrup, the ball of your foot should be resting on the stirrup tread.

REMEMBER this is your point of balance.

Try to feel the outside of your foot against your stirrup iron. This helps to keep your feet straight and secure. If your foot is too far forward or too far back, you will not be able to balance your weight over your foot.

REMEMBER your feet should face forward, just like your pony's feet.

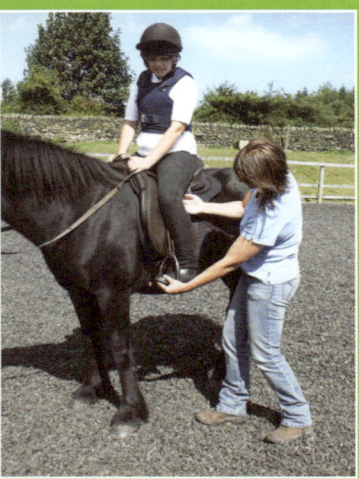

Ask your parent or guardian for help and feedback.

To put your foot in the correct position, your knee has to be flexible. If the back of your knee joint is too rigid or straight, your foot is pushed forward. You will be out of balance.
If your knee joint is too closed and tight your foot will be drawn up; you will be tipped forward causing you to be out of balance. Your knee joint should be flexible and springy.

think like a pony
IN THE SADDLE

To keep your knee joint flexible and open imagine there is a sponge ball behind your knee. Try to think that you can squeeze it but not flatten it.

If your toes are turned out, your knees and hips will be tight and your thigh and knee will be off your saddle. You will find it difficult to be in balance and move freely.
With your toes pointing forward your thigh will lie against your saddle and this helps to distribute your weight more evenly over your pony's back. This way you are more comfortable to carry.

If your hips are tight this will affect how you move in the saddle and how your leg hangs against your pony's side. To help you to become more flexible keep your feet flat in the stirrup, bend and flex from your hip and reach forward to stretch towards your pony's ears. Try to keep your bottom in the saddle and your feet parallel to the floor. This will help you to become flexible and supple in your hips so that you can move freely with your pony.

If your leg is too far back, it will be impossible for you to balance your weight over the balls of your feet because your toes will point down and you will put pressure on your pony's side.

Think Like a Pony, if you put constant pressure on his sides he will feel that you are nagging him. He will eventually ignore your legs.

REMEMBER how heavy you were when you sat out of balance on your partner's knee!

Check the length of your stirrups. Stand in your stirrups and balance on your knees. Make sure you don't tip forwards or backwards and your feet stay underneath your bottom.

Think of standing on the floor. Check that you have a small gap (big enough to put your clenched fist in) between you and the saddle. If your stirrups are too long you will more easily lose your balance. If they are too short, you may become tense and rigid.

If you need to, adjust the length of your stirrups now.

Sit down gently in the saddle and think about your upper body. Slouch in the saddle, it will feel as if your waist has disappeared.

In this position you are heavier in the saddle. Your shoulders are forward and you are out of balance. You may cause your pony to slouch.

Slowly sit up and think that your rib cage can grow up and out of your waist and your shoulder blades can slide and melt down your back.

Check that your neck is relaxed, smile and breathe. Think of your ears being over your shoulders. Your head is very heavy and when you move your head it will affect your balance and your pony's balance. If you stiffen your neck your body will become rigid and you will be more likely to fall off! You need to keep your body relaxed enough to move but firm enough to stay on.

If you stick your chest out you will hollow your back. This will affect how your spine moves and how you sit in the saddle. Your movement will be restricted. You need to allow your pony's movement through the whole body for you both to be able to move together and be comfortable.

think like a pony
IN THE SADDLE

When you are in balance in the saddle you will be lighter and your pony will be more comfortable.

When he is comfortable and you are balanced, it is easier for you to communicate with him and to influence his movements.

- You have to be able to carry your own weight as much as possible so that your pony can carry you comfortably.
- You must be balanced so that your pony can be balanced.
- You must be flexible and be able to move so that your pony can move.

If necessary, ask your helper to hold your pony so you can practise sitting in balance. Bring your arms out to the side, then down to rest behind your thighs. Breathe and relax without collapsing.

Lift your hands above your head, palms facing inwards. Be careful not to lift your shoulders.

Feel the stretch as your ribcage lifts up. Smile and breathe.

Be aware of your bottom in the saddle. Think that your bottom and legs can grow down, as your ribs float up. Your breathing can help you imagine this. Be aware of your knees resting against the saddle, keep them flexible, springy and soft.

Now bring your arms out to the side and down to rest behind your thighs. Breathe and relax without collapsing. You now should feel light and in balance.

Practise these movements as often as you can, so that you can feel what it is like to be light and balanced in the saddle.

Practise when you are not riding. Look at yourself in the mirror.
- What does it look and feel like when you think of lifting your ribcage?
- Can you lift your ribcage, relax your shoulders and keep breathing?

What does it look and feel like when you:
- Drop your ribcage?
- Close your chest?
- Imagine a smile across your chest?
- Force your shoulder blades back?
- Allow your shoulder blades to slide down your back?

Being aware of your body language will help to make you a better rider for your pony. Improving your balance and posture will help him to improve his posture and balance.

Chapter 12
Walk on and stop

Taking the time to build a language between you and your pony shows that you care. Allowing him time to make sense of your requests is considerate and respectful. This helps you to train your pony so that he can learn to respond to what you are asking. This is good leadership.

Take your time to understand how to use phases of signals to ask your pony to go and stop. This way your pony will learn to respond to your lightest aid. Riding will become fun for you and your pony.

Exercise 7: Asking your pony to walk on

With adult supervision, in a safe place where you both feel comfortable, tack up your pony and prepare to ride. When you are ready mount your pony.

1. Ask your helper to check your position in the saddle. Pick up your reins and hold them in front of your saddle.

Make sure your hands, arms and body are allowing your pony to move.

Think that you would like to move forward. Imagine your seat bones are lifting and walking forward.

think like a pony
IN THE SADDLE

> Let this feeling go all the way through your body, to your feet and hands. This is like a wave of energy moving forward.
>
> Imagine your arms can push your pony forward and your reins are like two sticks that will guide him. This is an imaginary push.

As you think and have an intention your body will start to prepare to go and your pony will be aware of this. He will feel you lighten in the saddle and feel your weight shift forwards. This may only be a very small change in your body language but your pony is very sensitive. If you are consistent and give him time to respond he will start to be aware of these small changes.

This is the first signal asking him to go.

Give him a few seconds to feel this before you give him the next signal.

He may not move forward from this intention today, but if you are consistent with your communication, one day he will!

2. **Allow this thought and intention to become an action and close your thighs against your saddle, just enough for your pony to feel it.**

   If you squeeze too hard you will tense your body. A tense body cannot move and your pony will become tense and he will feel like he cannot move.

   This is your second signal.
   Give him a few seconds to feel it.

If your pony responds and moves forward, release your pressure immediately and give him a rub on the withers. Allow him to walk forward. Allow him to lift and move you in the saddle and move with him. Imagine that your arms are elastic so that they can allow him to move forward. Follow this movement in your arms, shoulders and back. Think of 'pushing' arms and reins.

You will feel his head nod as he walks. He must be able to complete the nod of his head in order to complete his walk stride. If you restrict his head by holding the reins too tight you will restrict his walk, or even cause him to slow down and stop. Make sure you do not bring your elbows behind your body or your hands backwards behind the saddle.

3. If your pony does not walk forward then close your calf against his side. Have the feeling that you can push his skin forwards. Be careful not to draw your legs up or kick backwards towards his hindquarters. Keep your feet flat to the floor and toes pointing in the direction you want to go.

If your pony responds and moves forward immediately release the pressure from your legs. This is your third signal.
Allow your pony to move forward and give him a rub on his withers.

If you cannot feel this, ask your helper to put their hand under your calf. Close your leg gently against their hand and try to push their hand forward.

> When you have practised and felt this, try again without your helper.

4. If your pony does not respond to the feeling of pressure from your calf, check that you are not pulling back on the reins and you are breathing and balanced. If you are holding your breath you will become tense.

Now tap firmly with rhythm **on the girth** with one leg then the other. Be careful not to kick back towards his hindquarters. This is a polite firm tapping, not a kick. If he walks forward, stop tapping, release your pressure and allow him to move forward. This is your fourth signal. Give him a rub on the withers.

5. If your pony does not respond to tapping from your leg you can put both reins in one hand and hold them straight out in front of you. With your free hand, reach behind the saddle and tap. The moment he walks forward, stop tapping, release the pressure from your leg and allow your pony to walk forwards. This is your fifth signal. Give him a rub on the withers.

Make sure at all times you sit light in the saddle. Lifting your rib cage helps you to carry your own weight and allows your pony to lift his back so he can move. Remember to release the pressure from your leg. Keeping the pressure on, or using your legs constantly against his side, will make him dull.

The worst things that you can do to ask your pony to go are:
- Trying to urge him forward with your bottom. This will cause him to become tense and anxious. It is much better to communicate clearly and effectively.
- Kicking backwards towards his hindquarters. Pressure here is a signal to move his hindquarters away from you not forward. If you allow your legs to creep backwards and kick, your pony will become confused and you will be out of balance.

Using a stick
It may be necessary to use a stick to signal 'go forward' if:
- Your pony doesn't listen to your hand.
- You are small or cannot reach to tap behind the saddle.
- Or your helper needs to assist you.

Exercise 7a: Riding with a stick

Before you think about riding with a stick it is important to introduce your pony to it on the ground. If you are unsure how to do this see Think Like a Pony on the Ground Step 1. If you have never held a stick when riding keep your halter on underneath your bridle and ask your helper to hold the rope.

1. Show your pony the stick before you get on, rub him on his left and right side.

2. From the saddle show him the stick on his:
    Left and right shoulder.
    Left and right side of girth.
    Left and right hindquarter.

3. Make sure you can touch him with it, especially on his bum.

Try to scratch him with it.

If at any time he walks away, keep rubbing him with the stick until he stops.

When he does, stop rubbing and sit quiet and relaxed.

If he appears worried or unconfident go back to working on the ground. When he is more relaxed, try again from the saddle. He must be confident with the stick before you can use it to reinforce your leg aid.

REMEMBER a stick is just an extension of you!

When you can do this, get ready to ask him to walk forward.

You can either hold the reins in one hand and the stick in the other or hold one rein and stick together and the other rein in your free hand. Make sure that you do not pull back on the reins.

This time, instead of tapping with your hand, tap lightly and politely with rhythm, as near to your leg as you can. Keep up this tapping with the intention that you are irritating your pony, not hurting him.
There is no need to tap harder or faster, just be determined not to give in.

REMEMBER a small fly can cause him to move.

The moment your pony moves forward stop tapping and release the pressure from your leg. Allow your pony to walk forward and give him a rub on his withers.

To the parent or guardian:
If your child is small or unable to tap lightly with their leg or stick, tap the pony lightly on the hindquarters at the same time that they are squeezing forward with their calf. Be careful not to startle the pony and make sure he is prepared from the ground to understand your signals.

You now have phases of signals to go. These are called aids to go.
- **Your intention and thoughts.**
- **Your body language.**
- **Your leg aid.**
- **Your stick (or hand) aid.**

Your pony is now used to your phases of signals and will quickly learn to respond to the lightest aid.

This means you must always start light and be willing to reinforce your signals at any time.

If you are consistent and always reward your pony for doing the right thing he will be more willing to listen and respond to your requests. If you repeatedly nag or kick him, he will learn to ignore you. It is much better and kinder to teach your pony to listen to a light aid. By reinforcing your aids with a tap from your hand or stick, it shows your pony that you are willing to use phases of pressure until he responds.

REMEMBER ponies use phases of pressure with each other when they are resolving leadership issues. A good leader can politely and respectfully ask their pony to move forward.

If your pony trots, relax and breathe out. Use your body language to signal that you want him to walk by resisting his movement. Ask him to stop using one rein, making sure that you do not pull. If he does not respond, brace one hand and rein on your pony's neck.

With the other hand, ask your pony to flex his head and neck and wait for him to stop as you have practised before.

Occasionally check the girth as it may need to be tightened as your pony relaxes. Try to get into the habit of tightening your girth from both sides to keep the pressure equal.

You are now going to use your body language, weight and balance to signal to him that you want to slow down and stop.

If he ignores or does not understand these signals you will use a light pressure from your reins to ask him to slow down and stop.

By resisting his movement you can let him know that you want him to slow down and stop.

Exercise 7b: Asking your pony to stop

1. As your pony walks forward start to think that you would like him to slow down and stop. As you breathe out, imagine your out breath sinking down through your body and into the saddle, helping you to resist his movement and hold yourself still in the saddle. Make sure you lift your ribcage and feel your shoulder blades sliding down your back. This way you are light and he can lift his back to step under with his back legs.

This is your first signal.

2. Allow your thoughts to become an action and try to resist your pony's movement. As he tries to lift your seat bones forward, you can imagine you are going to reverse or stop your seat bones and resist his forward movement.

You can imagine that you are going to hold your body still without being tense or rigid. This gives your pony time to feel your body language before you use a rein aid. You must still allow your pony forward to step his hind legs underneath himself.

If you are tense then your pony will be tense, remember to breathe and smile. Try to breathe out through your transition from walk to stop.

It will help you to imagine that your legs and feet can reach for the ground, so that you can 'stop walking'. At the same time imagine you can grow up from your waist so that you remain light in the saddle.

Feel that you can spread your toes in your boots. This will also help you to keep your stirrups level and prevent your foot from shooting forwards or backwards.

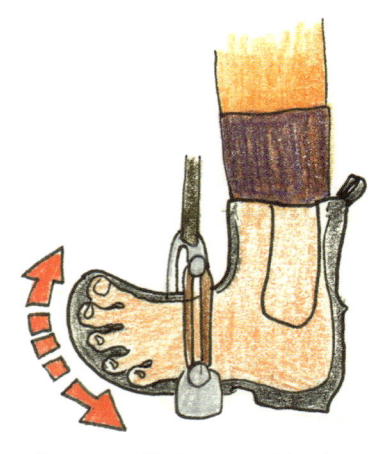

Imagine that you can drop an anchor from the ball of your foot to the ground, to signal that you want to stop.

Using you body language in this way is your second signal.

Be careful not to push your feet forward as this will affect your pony's balance and push your seat bones into the saddle. This may prevent your pony from lifting his back and stepping under with his hind legs.

You may feel your pony slow down his walk. That is excellent! He is trying to feel what you want him to do.

If he slows down and stops, give him a rub on the withers. Well done!

To get your pony to slow down and stop with you will take time, so be patient.

3. If he does not respond to you slowing down and resisting his movement then slowly close your fingers around the right rein. This will put a slight pressure on the rein. Remember to keep hold of the left rein. Only use the muscles in your hand so that you are not pulling back. Make sure that your elbow does not come behind your body and your hands stay in front of the saddle. Keep thinking that you want to stop.

This is your third signal to stop.

If he stops rub him and release the pressure from your rein.

4. If he keeps walking, use the muscles in your lower arm to increase the pressure and feel on the rein. Keep your thumbs on top of the reins so that they are secure. Think of your hands as a pair. When you look down they should look the same. Hold your intention to stop.

This is your fourth signal.

Make sure that you do not pull back on two reins or take your elbows behind your body and your hands stay in front of the saddle. If he stops give him a rub and release the pressure from the rein.

5. If he keeps walking use a light feel on the left rein to ask him to flex his head and neck a little to the left. This will help him to relax and encourage him to stop moving forwards.

This is your fifth signal.

Keep a hold of your right rein maintaining a light pressure to ask him to stop. There is no need to pull backwards as this will put too much pressure on your pony's head and mouth!

If your pony stops, release your feel on both reins and rub him on the withers. Sit still, breathe out and relax.

6. If your pony is still finding it difficult to slow down and stop, ask him to flex his head and neck a little more to the left. Keep hold of your right rein. Be careful not to pull backwards. Hold your intention to stop and resist his movement. Keep breathing.

This is your sixth signal.

7. If your pony will still not stop check that:

- Your reins are not too long, your hands are in front of the saddle, thumbs on top, hands a pair.
- You are resisting his movement but still allowing him to step under with his hind legs. If you sit too heavy he cannot do this.
- You are relaxing and breathing using your breath to help to hold you still in the saddle.

Brace your right hand as you have practised, against your pony's neck keeping hold of the right rein. Then ask your pony to flex his head and neck as far as he can around to look at your knee.
Keep breathing and try to resist his forward movement on every out breath.

This is your seventh signal.

Keep this flexion now until he stops, holding your right hand against his neck.
When he relaxes and stops release the pressure and rub him. Smile, well done!

This is the plan you would follow in an emergency if your pony would not stop. If you have had to flex your pony around as far as this to stop it means he is uncertain about what you are asking, or for some reason he cannot stop. He may be:
- Anxious
- Afraid
- In pain
- Trying to be the leader.

Think like a Pony. Check his body language to help you understand the problem.

Make sure that each time you ask him to slow down and stop you go through all the phases of signals.
a) Think and intend to slow down and stop.
b) Feel yourself resisting his movement. Allow him to step under with his hind legs.
c) Breathe out and relax.
d) Use your rein pressure in phases.
e) Make sure you use one rein to stop, the other rein to ask him to flex.
f) When you use your reins make sure you keep the feel of a shared contact between you and your pony.

If you always give your pony the same clear signals he will learn to stop on the lightest signal.

When you are both learning together you will need to wait a few seconds between each signal. When he understands more what you are asking and you are confident in the way you ask, you can ask him to stop more quickly.

The more you are aware of your pony's movement, the more you can move with him. Then he will be willing to move freely and stop and go when you ask.

If at any time your pony trots, go through your slow down and stop routine.

When he is relaxed try again to ask him to walk forward.

If he stops before you begin to ask him to, ask him to walk on immediately. Use phases as necessary. If you correct him quickly he will then understand that stopping is not the correct thing to do.

think like a pony
IN THE SADDLE

To the parent or guardian. If your child is young or not confident or your pony keeps trotting then all these exercises can be done on a halter and line for extra safety and confidence building.

If your pony acts dangerously at any time, seek professional help.

If he pulls on the reins or tries to pull the reins out of your hands, rest your hands on his neck. Be determined not to pull, if you pull him, he will pull you back. You may even teach him to pull. When he stops pulling, release the rein by offering them forward. Keep your fingers around the rein, your thumbs on top.

If you are consistent and practise using your intention first, slow down and give you and your pony time to think, he will eventually respond to your intention and thought.

Keep practising your phases of signals to ask your pony to go and stop. Be determined to think about what you are doing. This way you will be ready to make the correct response for your pony.

let's go!

Chapter 13
Moving together

When your pony walks there is a lot of movement. The barrel of his body swings from side to side as his hind legs move to step forward under his body and his shoulder blades roll up and forward as his front legs step forward. You can feel and see this. Try to watch your pony walk freely when you are not riding him.

You and your pony are trying to become a team, moving together as you ride. You are learning to influence your pony's movement and communicate with him through your thought, intention and body language.

You need to understand how much you can influence your pony's movement with your body language to prepare yourself for riding.

Try this: Feeling the walk

With a partner

1. One person is the pony. One person is the rider. Place your hands on your 'pony partner's' back. You are going to feel the movement in their back as they crawl slowly forward.

   Keep your hands light and fingers flat, so you can feel their movement through your hands.

2. Ask your partner to crawl slowly forward and follow their movement. Allow and feel this movement through your hands.

   Think Like a Pony, this is what it feels like to follow your pony's movement through your bottom when you ride.

3. As they move forward slowly try to keep your hands still and resist their forward movement.

What happens to your partner?

When you allow and follow the movement your partner can crawl freely forward. When you resist their movement your partner should feel like they want to stop.

Think Like a Pony, this is what it feels like when you resist your pony's movement with your body.

4. Ask your partner to crawl slowly forward again and this time move your hands in the opposite direction to try and move them backwards.

There is no need to press hard, just use as much feel and pressure as you need to influence their movement.

Your partner should feel that you want them to reverse or back up.

5. As your partner crawls slowly forward, put more weight in your right hand.

Your partner may now find it difficult to move the right side of their body.

Try the same with your left hand.

Think like a pony. This is what it could feel like if you were crooked when you sit on your pony's back.

6. Now put your hands around your partner's sides. Imagine this is where your legs would be in the saddle. Follow your partner's movement as they crawl slowly forward. Hold them lightly, keep in rhythm with their movement.

As they move slowly forward, start to squeeze and hold your hands against their side.

Does this have the effect of slowing them down or speeding them up?

Your partner may feel uncomfortable and want to stop.

Think like a pony. Legs that hold and squeeze when you are moving are uncomfortable and may stop your pony from wanting to move forward.

It is important to understand and feel this before you start to ride.

Make sure you swap over with your partner so that you can feel what it is like to be a 'pony'. These exercises are important so try them more than once.

Talk about them with your partner and your parent or guardian.

> When you allow your pony to move freely underneath you, you can use your body language to influence your pony's movements. Sitting on your pony should feel as if you are a team moving together in harmony. Your legs are your pony's legs and where you go, you go together.

Exercise 8: Following the walk as you ride

With adult supervision, in a safe place where you both feel comfortable, tack up your pony and prepare to ride.

When you are ready mount your pony.
- When you are safely mounted relax, check your balance and position.
- Are you carrying your own weight?
- Are your seat bones balanced over your feet?
- Are the reins the correct length?
- Are your hands in front of the saddle?
- Do you have a light contact on the reins?
- Ask your pony to walk forward.

1. As your pony is walking forward, sit quietly. Don't ask or kick back on every stride, just allow your pony's movement to naturally move your legs. Try to imagine your feet are walking on the ground as your pony is walking forward. Have the feeling in your hands, arms and shoulders that you are allowing your pony forward. If there is any backward feel on the reins or your body he will feel it. This may confuse him and he may try to slow down or stop.

2. Feel your pony move you in the saddle. As he walks, his barrel (the ribs of his body) moves from side to side. You can feel this against your legs. Look down at his shoulder. You will see his shoulder blades roll as he steps out with each front leg.

3. Think about the movement of your bottom in the saddle. You will feel your pony move the right side of your bottom upwards and forwards, then the left side of your bottom up and forwards.

4. Put both your reins in one hand. Your helper can hold your pony or walk at the side of you.

Place your free hand under your bottom where you touch the saddle.

Can you feel your seat bone?

REMEMBER these are the bones you balance on when you are sitting.

Your pony lifts each seat bone upwards and forwards in turn as he walks.

When you have felt one side, feel the other then hold the reins in two hands again. Notice what happens to your seat bones as your pony moves.

When one seat bone moves forward, the other is sliding back. When one is going up, the other is going down.

Be aware of your spine, you should be allowing this movement through your whole body.

Your weight should be equal in each seat bone, so it is easy for your pony to lift and move each one. If one seat bone is heavier it will be more difficult for him to move on that side.

If one seat bone is heavier then check that you are not leaning or collapsing your ribs to one side.

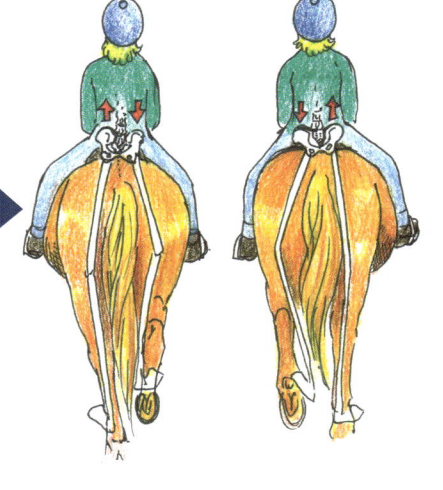

REMEMBER if your legs are too far forward or too far back it will affect your balance. If your upper body is too far forward, too far back, leaning or collapsed in any way, it will affect your balance over these seat bones.

Your balance and movement are important to:
• Allow your pony to move forward freely.
• To ask your pony to stop or go.

Bring your attention back to your bottom.

5. Now become aware of your legs. Each leg is moved in turn by your pony's barrel.

   You will feel your lower leg swing out and then in and your knee drop with each alternate stride. This is because your pony's barrel swings left then right with each step he takes.

   At walk: when his left hind foot comes off the ground, your pony's belly swings to the right. This shifts his weight so that he can now step forward with his left hind leg.

   At walk: when his right hind foot comes off the ground his barrel swings to the left.

As he does this he lifts you in the saddle. You need to be balanced to allow him to do this.

You must carry your own weight as much as possible so that your pony can move you in the saddle.

By allowing the movement of his barrel to move your seat bones, you can learn to follow his movement at walk.

If at any time your pony stops, go through your phases of signals to go, then try to get in rhythm with his walk.

To help you to feel this movement hold both your reins in one hand in front of the saddle. Check your reins stay the same length as your pony's neck and are allowing him forwards. If you want, your parent or guardian can lead you.

Make sure you stay relaxed so that your body does not become rigid and difficult to move. Keep smiling and breathing. Smiling helps you to relax.

6. Now place one hand straight up above your head with your palm facing inward. This lifts your ribcage on that side and lightens your seat. You should now be able to feel your seat bone more easily.

As you stretch up, imagine feeling for the ground with your feet and that you allow your leg to lengthen. Just think about this and allow it to happen. If you try to force it you will become stiff and rigid. Feel your knee drop in the saddle, first one side then the other. Make sure you breathe and smile.

When you have felt one side, swap hands.

When your pony's barrel moves against your legs it should feel equal on both sides and you should feel your knee drop equally on both sides.

If the movement of his barrel is not equal it means he is not stepping under as far with one hind leg.

This may be because:
- **His front leg is not stepping out.**
- **His saddle may be restricting his movement.**
- **You may be restricting his movement.**
- **He may be tight or sore somewhere over his back or in his hind leg.**

Ponies can quickly get into the habit of walking incorrectly, just like you!
You can encourage him to walk correctly by thinking about your seat bones lifting left then right in the saddle. Imagine that you can encourage his barrel to swing by allowing your knee to drop in the saddle. You can imagine reaching for the floor as his barrel moves away from your leg. At the same time think about him lifting you up and forward in the saddle, first one side, then the other. Think about growing up from your hips and down from your legs.

As you think about these things you will encourage him to walk freely.

> You only need to think about this. If you start to do too much in the saddle you may upset his rhythm and balance and confuse him.

When you can follow the walk it becomes easier to influence your pony to stop and go or speed up and slow down. You should never have to kick your pony to go.

You can help your pony to be more aware of your body language by slowing down and speeding up. This also helps to get your pony thinking and can improve his balance and rhythm.

Exercise 8a: Speeding up and slowing down

1. **As your pony walks forward, start to think that you would like to walk faster. Think of your seat bones lifting up and forwards a little quicker.**

**Think of your legs encouraging his barrel to swing away from your legs.
Feel that you can use your legs individually. First one leg then the other.**

If necessary, give him a gentle forward nudge with one leg then the other. As soon as your pony responds, stop nudging. This way he knows he has done the right thing. If you nudge on every stride, he will quickly ignore your leg or feel that you are restricting him from walking forward. Be careful not to nudge him too hard or your pony may think you want him to trot. If you feel you pony is about to trot, slow down your body, breath out, relax then try again.

Remember the exercise you did with your partner. Make sure you look up and have the intention you want to go somewhere. Be smiley and enthusiastic!!

2. When you feel him speed up he should be taking bigger strides. Try to offer one rein forward and rub him on his withers and keep 'walking' with him.

3. Walk like this for a short time then imagine you would like to walk slower.

Feel you can slow down your seat bones to a slow walk.

4. Allow your thoughts to become an action and try to resist your pony's movement as he tries to lift your seat bones forwards.

5. Imagine that you are going to hold your body still without being tense or rigid. Hold the reins and make sure that you are not pulling the reins back. You must still allow your pony forward to step his hind legs underneath himself.

If you are tense then your pony will be tense, remember to breathe and smile.

6. It will help you to imagine that your legs and feet can reach for the ground, so that you can 'stop walking'. At the same time imagine you can grow up from your waist so that you remain light in the saddle.

think *like a pony*
IN THE SADDLE

Feel that you can spread your toes in your boots. This will also help you to keep your stirrups level and prevent your foot from shooting forwards or backwards.

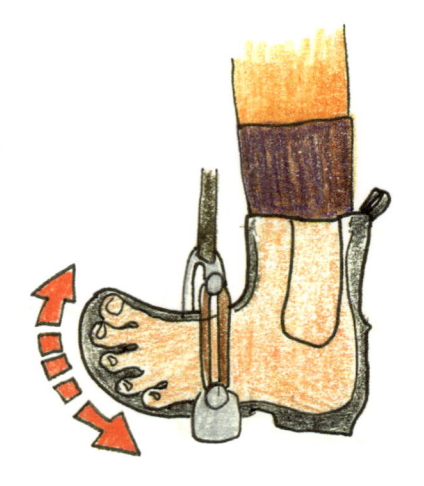

Imagine that you can drop an anchor from the ball of your foot to the ground, to signal that you want to slow down.

When you feel your pony slow down his walk, well done! He is trying to feel what you want him to do.

You can experiment with how little it takes to slow your pony down and speed him up or even stop, without using the reins.

To get your pony to slow down and stop with you will take time so be patient with yourself and your pony.

7. When you can feel him walk slowly, offer one rein forward and give him a rub to tell him he has done the right thing. Keep 'walking' with him.

8. How slow can you walk without stopping?

9. How fast can you go without trotting?

Get in time with each other and have fun!

Chapter 14
Using your body language to direct your pony

When you ride you need to direct your pony where you want to go. If you cannot direct your pony, then he will think he is the leader and try to take over.

REMEMBER it is important that you are your pony's leader to be in control and help him feel safe and secure. If you pull him around to 'steer' him, he will become afraid, confused or tense. To help your pony to become a happy, willing partner you have to use your body language correctly to control and direct him, before you use the reins. When you use your body language correctly he can more easily make sense of what you are asking and he can then relax.

You are going to work with a partner to feel what it may be like being ridden and directed and prepare yourself to ride your pony.

Try this: Directing your partner!

1. One person is going to be the pony.
   One person is going to be the rider.

2. Straddle your 'pony partner's' back, stand up straight, your legs just lightly by their sides, your feet facing forwards.

   Ask your partner to relax their head and neck by looking down at the floor.

   Balance yourself over the balls of your feet, with your feet facing forwards. Hold your arms as if you are holding the reins.

3. Now turn your eyes, nose, shoulders and belly button slowly to the left.

As you turn your partner should turn.

Now repeat this to turn to the right.

Your partner should easily turn to the left and the right following your body language.

Repeat this exercise trying to:

- Turn your toes out like a duck. Now try to move your partner to the left or right. Is it easy to turn your partner?

- Turn your feet in. Can you turn your partner?

- Just turn your eyes and nose. Can you turn your partner?

- Just turn your shoulders. Can you turn your partner?

- Now turn your eyes, nose, shoulders and belly button to the left and ask your partner to try to move to the right. They will find it very difficult.

Swap over so that you have a chance to feel what it is like to be a 'pony'.

think like a pony
IN THE SADDLE

Think Like a Pony, if you learn to use your body language correctly your pony will learn to follow your directions.

When you ride your pony you have a leg on either side of his body. When you want to walk straight forward together, think of asking your pony to move in between your legs and hands, your belly button pointing forward between your pony's ears helping to direct him.

Imagine that your legs are like a 'tunnel' and your pony moves between them. Your belly button is a light beam showing the way.

> **Think of your pony 'flowing and moving' between your hands and legs.**

When you want to change direction, turning your eyes, nose, shoulders and belly button affects your legs.

As the 'tunnel' that your legs have created moves, you can guide your pony to move through this 'tunnel'. This tunnel is affected by your feet because your feet affect your bottom. Where your feet point your pony will go.

> **Practise turning your eyes, nose, shoulders and belly button together so that you can influence your pony's movement.**

It is important to be able to feel what is happening on both sides of your pony's body so that you can contain him in your 'tunnel' and direct his movements.

You should be aware of what is happening in your body and your pony's body so that you can easily and accurately move together. Knowing where your eyes, nose, belly button and legs are helps you to do this.

Exercise 9: Learning to direct your pony

With adult supervision, in a safe place where you both feel comfortable, tack up your pony and prepare to ride. When you are ready mount your pony.

1. Check your balance and position.

2. Ask your pony to walk forward and follow the rhythm and movement of his walk with your body and your reins.

3. Check the length of your reins and that you have a shared contact with your pony.

4. Look straight through the tip of your pony's ears, to a point in the distance where you will be walking in the next moment. Imagine your chest has eyes too!

think like a pony
IN THE SADDLE

5. Hold the reins lightly with a contact. Make sure they do not slip through your fingers and there is no backwards feel on the reins or in your body.

Check your feet are pointing forwards.

6. Now look up and start to turn your eyes, nose, shoulder and belly button to the right.

Imagine the eyes in your chest turning at the same time as the eyes in your head.

7. If your pony does not follow your body language, slowly lift your rein up and out to the right to open the rein. Imagine that you are 'opening the door' to show your pony where you want him to go. If you want to, you can point in the direction you want to go. Keep hold of the rein.

Your nose and hand should look up and over your right rein. Your rein position and body language should look the same.

The moment your pony responds to the feel on the rein that is directing him to turn, put your right hand down and back into neutral at the withers. Give him a rub.

Look forward over your pony's ears.

8. If your pony does not turn then open your rein a little more and lift your hand a little higher. Look up over your hand, making sure you turn to look with your eyes, belly button and shoulders.

Remember looking up will put your weight in the right place so that your pony can move his leg easily.

If your pony responds to the feel of your rein directing him to turn, lower your hand and put your rein back into neutral at the withers. Give him a rub and look over his ears to where you want to go to next.

When you can direct your pony to the right, then practise directing him to the left and use the left rein to help you.

Practise:
- Walking in a straight line
- Directing your pony to turn to the left
- Walking in a straight line
- Directing your pony to turn to the right

REMEMBER to use your intention and body language before your reins. Make sure you put your reins back into neutral at the withers when your pony has done the correct thing.

If you practise this pattern you will soon be using your reins less, if you are consistent with your body language. It will look and feel as if you are moving together. Riding becomes fun and natural and this way you and your pony become a team.

Being aware of your body language
You need to be able to use your hands and legs independently. This may be difficult because you will have one dominant hand or leg. This is the hand or leg that you prefer to use.
To improve your co-ordination, strength and awareness of how you use your body try to use your hands and legs equally in everyday tasks. This will help to develop even muscle tone and your overall flexibility.

If you are left handed use your right hand.
If you are right handed use your left hand to:
- Open doors.
- Brush your teeth.
- Comb your hair.
- Catch or throw a ball accurately.
- Use a bat or club.

Try to use both legs equally and alternate which:
- Shoe or sock you take off first.
- Leg you put into your trousers first.
- Foot you kick a ball with.

Notice how this feels and keep practising to improve your co-ordination.

Becoming athletic

Most people are more flexible on one side or more balanced on one side. Be aware of this and try to do as many varied things as you can to improve your flexibility and balance.

Can you:
- Touch your toes?
- Stand on one foot and stay in balance over the foot on the floor?
- Stand on one foot and try to tie or untie your shoelace?
- Reach over your shoulders and your back to touch the fingers on your opposite hand?

Try swapping hands or feet, does it feel the same both ways?

Keep working on your balance and flexibility so that you are as equal on both sides as you can be. This will help you to communicate more easily when you ride your pony.

If you want your pony to be:
- Supple
- Athletic
- Relaxed
- Calm
- Brave

you need to practise these qualities in everything you do.

Chapter 15
Moving backwards

Asking your pony to step backwards is very important because it helps to:
- **strengthen him.**
- **straighten him.**
- **improve his ability to stop.**

To move backwards correctly, your pony needs to move his weight back whilst lifting up his back and lowering his head and neck. If your pony sticks his head in the air he will not be able to use his back correctly. He may take backwards steps but he will be uncomfortable and this will be a bad experience for him.

Your pony uses different muscles to move backwards than when he moves forwards. These muscles also help him to stop in balance.

The better he backs up, the better he stops.

When your pony steps backwards correctly he uses diagonal pairs of feet.

As he steps backwards:
   His left front leg and right hind leg take the weight together.

As he takes his next step backwards:
   His right front leg and left hind leg take the weight together.

When your pony walks forward you will feel your pony lift your seat bones up and forwards, first one then the other.

When your pony steps backwards you will feel your pony lift your seat bone up and backwards, first one then the other.

When you learn to get in time with this movement you and your pony will find backing up easier.

Your pony will find it very difficult to move backwards if you are giving him mixed signals. You may think that you are asking him to back up, but your body language may be asking him to go forward or stop. If this happens you will have to rely on your reins to pull him back. This is not polite or fair and will cause your pony to become resistant.

Try this: Thinking backwards

Stand with your feet facing forwards and your legs hip width apart. Make sure your shoulders are relaxed, lift your ribcage and remember to breathe! Look straight ahead.

Bring your thoughts and intention to your belly button and chest by placing your fingers on your belly button. Think that you can lift your belly button and chest and move them backwards together. Keep looking straight ahead towards the horizon. As you move your belly button and chest backwards your weight will shift into your heels. Your toes will lift off the floor and you will have to step backwards to balance yourself.

Make sure that you are not leaning forward. If you lean forward you will re-balance yourself and your weight will not shift.

Practise this as much as you can without your pony, so that your body language signals are clear when you ride him.

Exercise 10: Asking your pony to step backwards when you ride him

In a place where you and your pony feel safe and comfortable, with adult supervision, tack up your pony and prepare to ride.

1. Before you get on make sure that your pony can step backwards from a gentle feel of backward pressure on the bit or bridle, as you have done before.

REMEMBER if your pony's head is about the level of his withers, he can back up comfortably.

2. When you are confident that your pony understands this, mount up.

   When you are ready ask him to walk forward and stop. Repeat this a couple of times to make sure he is listening to you.

3. As you stop think about asking your pony to take a step backwards.

   Lift your belly button and chest and move them backwards together. Keep looking straight ahead towards the horizon.

   Feel you weight shift backwards. Imagine lifting and reversing your seat bones.

All of this helps to make you light in the saddle, so that your pony can lift his back and step backwards with you.

This is your first signal.

If your pony backs up, stop asking and reward him.

4. If he does not back up give a gentle steady feel on one rein then the other to ask your pony to take a step backwards.

Use the left rein to ask his left front foot and right hind to take a step back.

Use the right rein to ask his right front foot and left hind to take a step back.

Try to think of getting in time with your reins and your body. Your left rein with your left seat bone, your right rein with your right seat bone.

This is your second signal.

The moment your pony responds and takes a step backwards, stop asking, even if he only steps back with one foot. Relax your body and pressure on the rein and give him a rub.

If your pony does not respond, check the length of the reins. If they are too long your pony will not be able to feel the steady pressure asking him to step backwards. The reins do not need to be short but it is important that they are not so long that you need to bring your arms behind your body.

5. If your pony does not respond, widen your hands. This stops you from pulling and taking your arms behind your body. Make sure that the reins do not slip through your hands by keeping your thumbs on top and your hands a pair. Keep asking your pony to step backwards with your intention and body language.

This is your third signal.

think *like a pony*
IN THE SADDLE

The moment he steps back, stop asking, relax and give him a rub.

6. If your pony does not respond, and you have checked your intention, position and body language, ask your helper to use rhythmic signals to remind him to listen to you.

These signals can come from a rope, stick, their hand or leg. It does not matter which, as long as the signals have phases and are rhythmical.

This is the fourth signal.

The moment he responds, stop asking. Give him a rub. Wait a few moments, then ask him again to step backwards.

Repeat this until he can back up without the use of rhythmic signals or pressure on the fiador knot.

This takes time so be patient with yourself and your pony.

The worst thing you can do is pull on the reins or give up.

> Giving up will show him that you are not a determined leader. Pulling will show him that you are not patient.

If at any time he puts his head in the air or opens his mouth check that you are not pulling. Your pony may also be putting his head in the air to avoid backing up because he has become tense or is unsure.

If he raises his head above his withers use one rein at a time to ask him to lower his head and neck before you continue to back up.

Ask for a little flexion one way, stop, then ask for a little flexion the other way then your pony will eventually learn to relax and will lower his head and neck.

You can ask your helper to do this from the fiador knot.

REMEMBER lowering his head and neck helps him to relax then he can use his back comfortably.

If he finds backing up difficult, look at his body language to try to understand why. He must be comfortable and pain free so that he can move backwards willingly.

If he shows signs of pain, stop and seek professional help.

If your pony is being resistant it is important to remind him that he can move backwards. Go back to working on the ground. When you are confident that he understands then ride him again.

As you and your pony learn to back up together you can start to be aware of his front legs moving. As you feel them move say out loud "left leg, right leg, left leg, right leg" and so on.

You will feel and hear the rhythm as you get in time with him. Allow your pony to lift you in the saddle as he steps backwards. If you get in time with your pony's feet with your body language and rein then backing up becomes easy, flowing and natural.

When you have felt his front legs move back in rhythm, you can get in time with this rhythm with your reins. Left rein, left leg, right rein, right leg and so on. Make sure that your contact on the rein does not pull him back, but is in time with the lift of his legs with a lift of the rein.

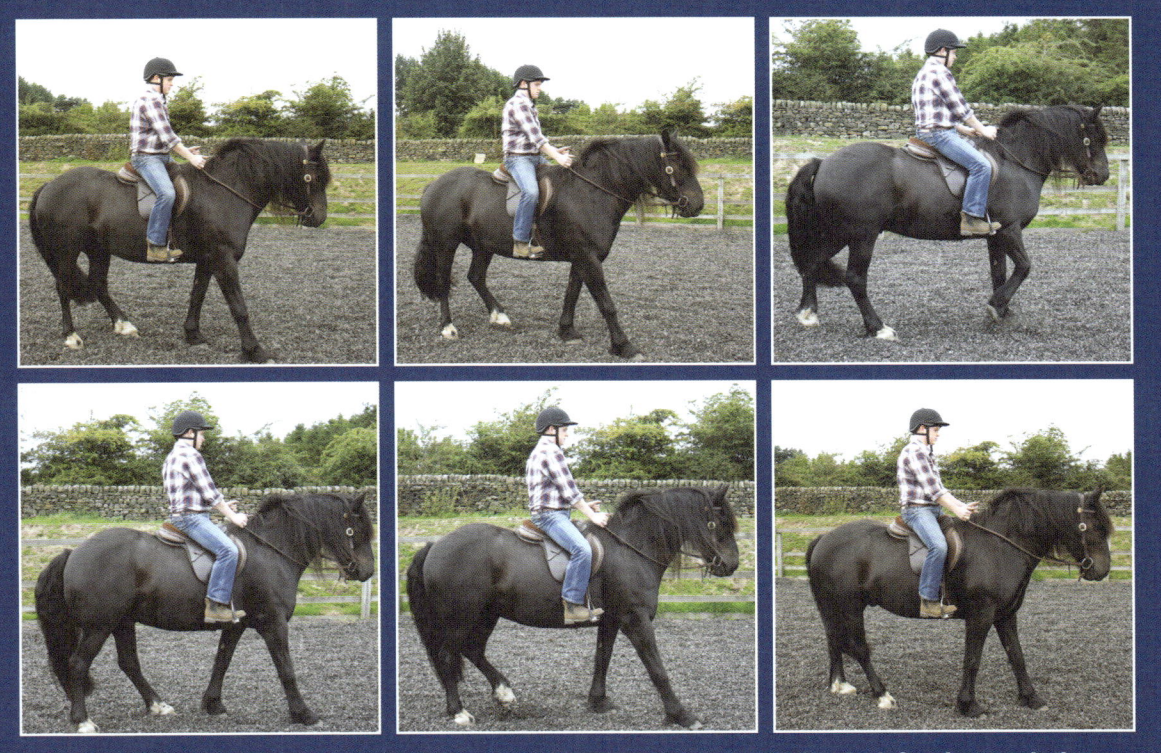

This way you will begin to feel that you can use your reins independently, left rein to ask the left leg back, right rein to ask the right leg back.

When you have felt this, stop and give him a rub.

If you still cannot get in time with his feet as he moves backwards, ask your parent or guardian to help you. If they ask your pony to step back, you can concentrate on the movement and your body language. This makes it easier to be aware of what is happening underneath you. If you want, ask your guardian to point when each front leg is moving.

Keep practising: Walk forwards;
                   Stop;
                   Step backwards and get in time with his front feet.

REMEMBER moving backwards can be very tiring. So keep the number of backward steps to a maximum of 12.

Reward him often and walk forward before you try again.

Think Like a Pony, difficult exercises are only fun if you can do them and you do not do them all the time! Practise just a few steps whenever you can.

REMEMBER the better you both can back up, the better you can stop. Backing up helps to make your pony athletic.

Chapter 16
Obstacles and challenges

To build your pony's trust and confidence, you are going to ask him to manoeuvre through, over and around obstacles.

When he is aware of things behind, around him and underneath him he will learn to manoeuvre slowly without panicking.

This helps him to be brave when you ride him through narrow spaces or you are getting ready to jump. This is also essential preparation for loading and unloading into a trailer or horsebox.

Remember, when a pony acts on their instinct they run first, and think second.

You want your pony to be a safe, thinking pony.

Working with poles
From the exercises that you have done before, you can confidently walk your pony over a pole on the ground. Now you're preparing your pony to:
- Walk over a pole.
- Stop over a pole.
- Back up over a pole.

Before you ride this exercise, you must check that your pony can stop and back over a pole confidently from the ground.

Exercise 11: Backing over a pole from the ground

With adult supervision, in a safe place where you both feel comfortable, with the halter on and the rope line attached.

1. Stand at your pony's shoulder and ask him to walk forward. Lead your pony forward and together walk over the pole as you have done before. If you need a reminder go back to Think Like a Pony on the ground, book 3, chapter 8.

2. Still at his shoulder turn around and bring him back to the pole. This time ask him to stop over the pole and give him a rub. Repeat this until your pony is confident and is not rushing.

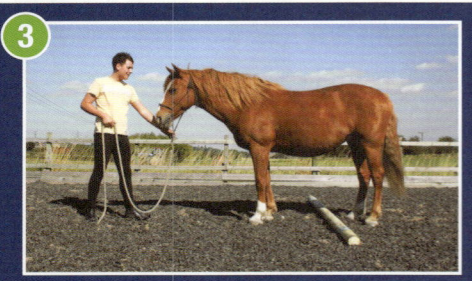

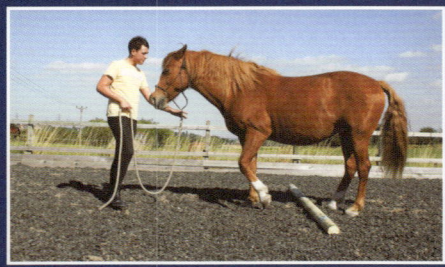

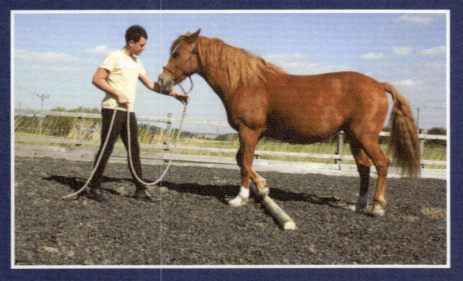

3. Come back and stop over the pole. This time stand in front of your pony and turn to face him. Use a feel of steady pressure on the fiador knot to ask him to step one front foot backwards over the pole. Make sure he is relaxed and he lowers his head and neck. Repeat this sequence a few times so he feels both front feet step backwards over the pole.

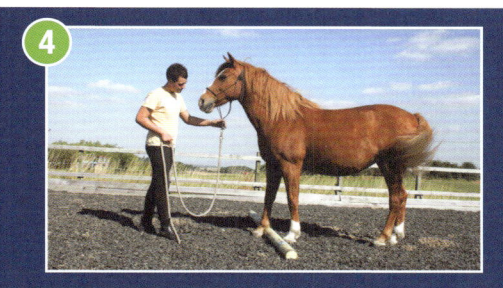

4. When he can do this confidently, ask one leg forward so the pole is between his front feet and stop.

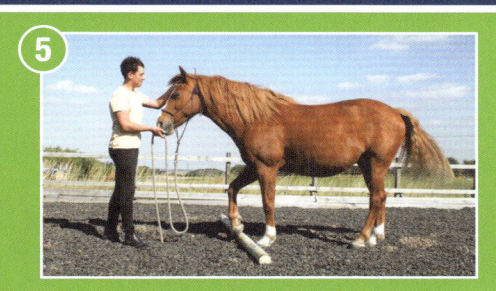

5. Ask him forward and repeat the sequence a few times. Give him time to feel confident with one foot over the pole then ask him to step backwards.

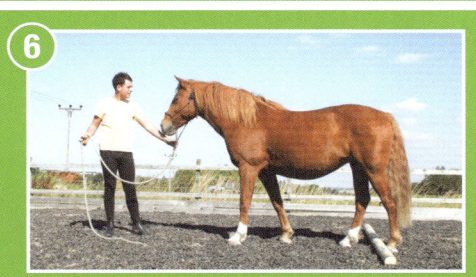

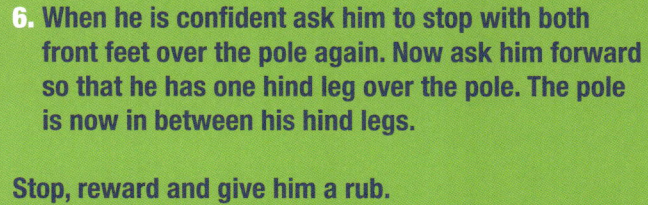

6. When he is confident ask him to stop with both front feet over the pole again. Now ask him forward so that he has one hind leg over the pole. The pole is now in between his hind legs.

Stop, reward and give him a rub.

When you are ready use a feel of steady pressure and ask him to step his hind leg back over a pole so that the pole is now under his belly.

Repeat this so he feels both hind feet step forwards and backwards over the pole.

think like a pony
IN THE SADDLE

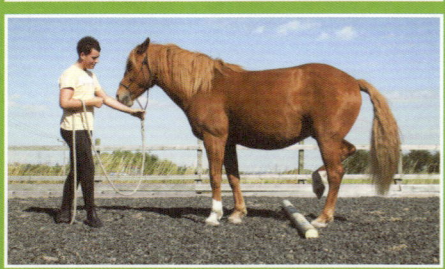

7. When you are ready ask both his hind feet to step forward over the pole and stop and reward him. Then use a feel of steady pressure to step both his hind feet backwards over the pole. First one then the other.

If he hesitates, reward each time he tries to lift his leg backwards over the pole. This way he will not feel rushed, he has time to think and you will help build his confidence.

If necessary be prepared to approach and retreat going back to walking over the pole, stopping and stepping his front feet backwards.

If at any time he rushes or seems scared, try to understand why by looking at his body language.

Are you:
- Asking too much too fast?
- Giving him time to think?
- Rewarding him often?
- Using approach and retreat to build his confidence?

If he does not move straight, as he backs over the pole, then check:
- You are standing squarely in front of him.
- You are not pushing him left or right.
- You are not flexing his head and neck to the left or right and causing him to be crooked as he moves backwards.
- You are giving him time to think.

154

If he moves his hindquarter to the left, step to your left and keep asking him to move backwards.

If he moves his hindquarter to the right, step to the right and keep asking him to move backwards. Make sure you keep his head in the centre of his chest so that you are moving his whole body backward. This will help to keep him straight.

If he still refuses to step backwards, then use rhythmic pressure on his chest to remind him to listen to the steady pressure from the halter.

You do not have to use a lot of rhythmic pressure, be gentle. Just irritate him enough to cause him to move then, reward him. Even if he just offers to move by picking up a leg to move backwards, reward him, because he is trying.

When your pony can do this exercise on the ground confidently, you are ready to ride forwards and backwards over a pole.

Exercise 11a: Riding forwards and backwards over a pole

With adult supervision, in a safe place where you both feel comfortable, tack up your pony and prepare to ride. When you are ready mount your pony.

1. When you are ready ask him to walk forward over the pole.

2. Turn around and come back over the pole.

Repeat this pattern a few times. If your pony lowers his head as he walks over the pole, that is excellent. Make sure you allow him to lengthen his neck by offering the rein forward. Keep your thumbs on top so that the reins do not slip through your hand.

As he lowers his head and neck, he is stretching his back and showing you that he is aware of the pole.

3. Turn to walk over the pole again, but this time as you approach it, have the intention that you want to stop over the pole.

Give your pony time to feel your intention.

As your pony is about to step his front feet over the pole signal him to stop.

When he stops reward him and give him a friendly scratch on his withers then walk on.

4. If he does not stop over the pole, ask him to keep walking and approach the pole again. Think about stopping earlier so that he has longer to feel your signals.

Be determined to stop, make sure your signal and body language are clear. Do not pull or you will cause him to be resistant.

Reward him when he stops over the pole.

If he only puts one foot over the pole that is ok, rest, give him a friendly scratch then walk on. Repeat this to build up his confidence.

If he is still not listening and stopping over the pole you can put his halter on and ask an adult to help you. When you are both confident, try again on your own.

5. When he can stop over the pole ask him to take a step backwards. This time he will move his front feet backwards over the pole.

Repeat this pattern until you are sure he is confident.

6. Approach the pole again and stop over the pole. This time ask him to step one hind foot over the pole. Stop, reward him, smile and relax.

This is fun, so be patient and make sure you both enjoy the exercise.

7. When you can do this stop and reward him. Wait a few moments. Smile and relax. Now ask him to step backwards. This time he will move three feet backwards over the pole.

Repeat this pattern a few times.

8. When you are both confident, have the intention to stop just after the pole.

Wait and rest here for a few moments and smile. Now have the intention that you want him to step backwards over the pole. Ask him to take a step backwards and get in time with his feet.
- **Take one step and wait.**
- **Next step, wait.**
- **Next step, wait.**
- **Last step, give him a big rub.**

Use your thought, intention, body language, weight and reins to achieve this!

It does not matter how long it takes, just keep having fun together, be calm and determined and you will succeed!

When you can step backwards over a pole, you can introduce other challenges. Start these challenges from the ground.

Try walking backwards, forwards and stopping:
- Through and around obstacle fillers or a pole tunnel.
- Through a gateway.
- Over a tarpaulin.

Walk through the obstacle.

Stop and back through the obstacle.

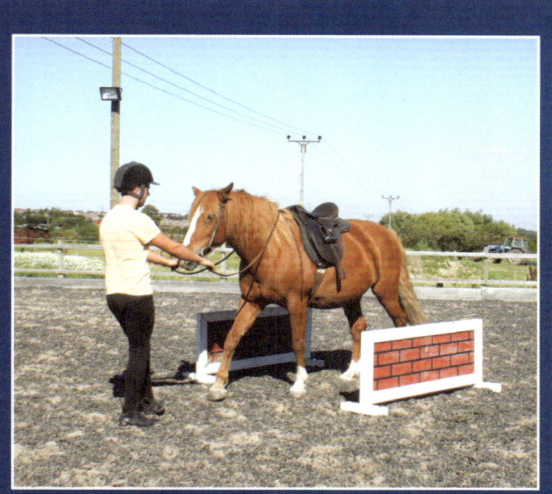

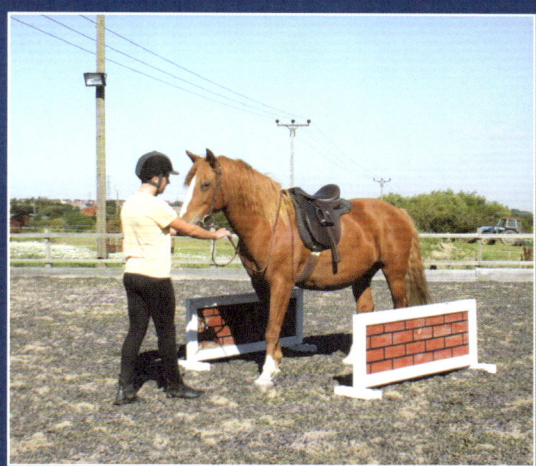

Forward and back through the obstacle.

Ride forward and back through the obstacle.

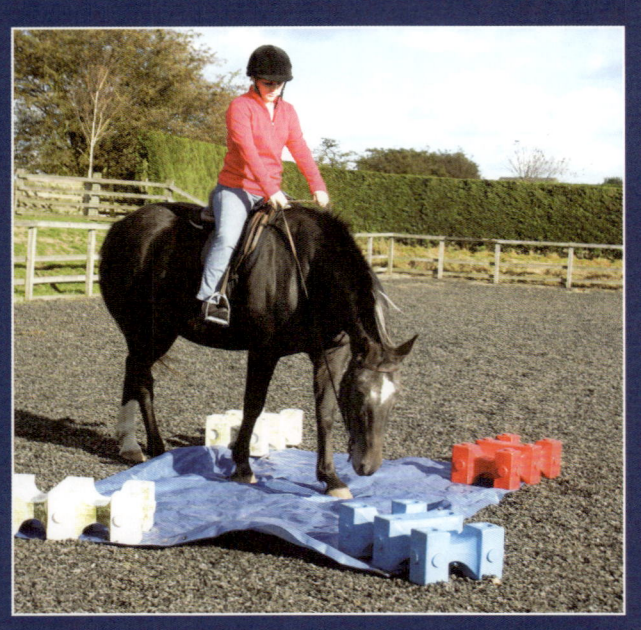

Make sure he is ok with the object.
Use approach and retreat at any time.

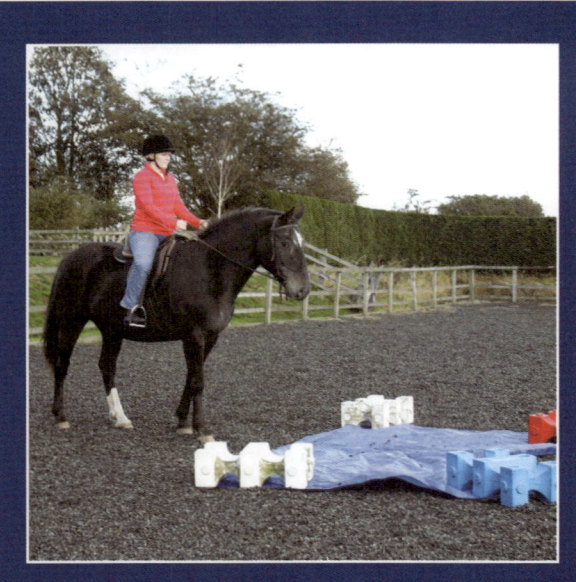

Approach and on!

Stop.

Back.

think like a pony
IN THE SADDLE

Thank you!

think *like a pony*
IN THE SADDLE

To the parent or guardian:
If your child or pony are not confident keep the halter on under the bridle and use the rope to support them until they both feel brave enough to face the challenge alone.

Be imaginative for your pony so that you can have fun together. Introducing safe challenges helps to develop your pony's curiosity and motivates him to learn about his environment. You want your pony to be interested and willing to do things with you. When you are introducing your pony to obstacles or challenges, he may hesitate, rush, or refuse to go forward.

You must learn to use approach and retreat as you ride him, to help him to build his confidence in any situation and in you. This is excellent preparation for hacking out or competitions when an unexpected obstacle may spook or scare your pony.

If he hesitates or stops:

Ask him forward making sure that you are not pulling back or kicking him behind the drive line. The moment he tries to move forward in the direction that you want, stop asking and reward him.

Be prepared to stand quietly in front of the object then your pony will have time to think and will not feel rushed.
Wait a few moments and ask him forward again. The moment he tries, stop asking and reward him. Repeat this until he can move forward in the direction that you want.

When he is moving in the direction you want, relax your legs. If you keep asking him forward he will feel rushed and may even become afraid.

Make sure you keep your intention and keep looking where you want him to go. A good leader focuses on where they are going.

If he changes direction away from the object:

Use your intention and body language first. Keep focused on where you want to go.

Use your reins independently to ask him to keep looking in the correct direction towards the object.

Give him time to look at the obstacle and think. Allow him to sniff it if he wants to.

If you can ask him to turn and face the obstacle he knows you can control his feet. He knows you are the leader!

When he can face the obstacle, make sure you relax and reward him. Give him time to think. Ask him to do one thing at a time. This way he can make sense of what you are asking and he will learn to listen to you.

If he moves backwards:

Keep asking him forward. Think forward and keep your aids for 'go forward' on.

If it is safe to do so, allow him to move backwards, but the moment he moves forwards again, stop asking and reward him. This way he knows that you will only stop asking him to do something when he does the correct thing and tries to go forward.

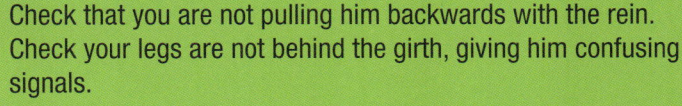

Check that you are not pulling him backwards with the rein. Check your legs are not behind the girth, giving him confusing signals.

If your pony still refuses to go forwards put the reins in one hand and tap him behind the saddle to ask him forward. The moment he responds stop and reward him. Be prepared to make the obstacle simpler to build his confidence.

If he keeps moving backwards when you want him to go forward, get off and show him from the ground what you want. Put his halter on if you need to and help him not to be afraid.

think like a pony
IN THE SADDLE

Keep your pony interested by being fun for him.

While you are having fun you are learning to:

- Stop where you want.
- Go where you want.
- Go around things.
- Go through things.
- Go over things.
- Turn when you want.

You are helping him to become confident, supple and relaxed.
Above all you are showing your pony that you care.